The 2,000 Year-Old Preacher:

21st-Century Sermons On 1st-Century Texts

Cycle B Sermons for Advent, Christmas, and Epiphany Based on the Gospel Texts

DAVID E. LEININGER

CSS Publishing Company Inc.
Lima, Ohio

The 2,000 Year-Old Preacher: 21st Century Sermons on 1st Century Texts

FIRST EDITION
Copyright © 2020
by CSS Publishing Co., Inc.

Library of Congress Cataloging-in-Publication Data:

Leininger, David E., 1944- author.
Title: The 2,000 year-old preacher : 21st century sermons on 1st century texts : Cycle B sermons for Advent, Christmas, and Epiphany based on the gospel texts / David E. Leininger.
Other titles: Two thousand-year-old preacher Description: First edition. | Lima, Ohio : CSS Publishing Company, Inc., 2020. | Summary: "Cycle B Lectionary Sermons for the Advent, Christmas, and Epiphany season based on the Gospel Texts"-- Provided by publisher.
Identifiers: LCCN 2020007255 | ISBN 9780788030109 (paperback) | ISBN 9780788030116 (ebook) Subjects: LCSH: Bible. Gospels--Sermons. | Common lectionary (1992). Year B.| Advent sermons | Christmas sermons | Epiphany--Sermons. Classification: LCC BS2555.54 .L45 2020 | DDC 252/.61--dc23 LC record available at https://lccn.loc.gov/2020007255
For more information about CSS Publishing Company resources, visit our website at www. csspub.com, email us at csr@csspub.com, or call (800) 241-4056.

e-book:
ISBN-13: 978-0-7880-3011-6
ISBN-10: 0-7880- 3011-6

ISBN-13: 978-0-7880-3010-9
ISBN-10: 0-7880-3010-8   DIGITALLY PRINTED

For my wonderful young Grandson
Noah Paul Padgett
and his new twin brothers
Davis Christopher Padgett and Ryan Daniel Padgett
in the hope that these timeless texts and stories
will become as precious to them
as they have been for so long to their PopPop.

Contents

Foreword

In the venerable phrasing of the King James Version of scripture in which my generation was nurtured, "...in the wisdom of God the world by wisdom knew not God, it pleased God by the foolishness of preaching to save them that believe" (I Cor. 1:21). The "foolishness of preaching?" I confess that in three-quarters of a century of churchthat I have witnessed, I have heard some pretty foolish preaching a time or two, but, on the whole, I have heard some pretty great preaching as well.

Sometime back someone sent me the biographical sketch of a man, the Rev. Samuel Suther, a minister of the German Reformed Church in North Carolina in pre-revolutionary days. He was born in Switzerland in 1722 and emigrated to America in 1739. Apparently, he was quite the firebrand in advocating a break with the English king, and as such, got himself in all sorts of difficulties. He sounded like an interesting character, but I doubt that I would have given him much more than passing thought except for the fact that there was included in his story a list of his children. It turns out that Rev. Samuel Suther was my great-great-great grandfather. That knowledge puts no money in my pocket, no eggs on my table; it accords me no special honor... but I am glad to have it. It gives me a sense of my own roots... who I am and from whence I have come ...and is another reminder that preaching runs in the family.

I am blessed to be able to lay additional claim to a legacy of distinguished preaching. Uncle Gil was better known as the Rev. Dr. Gilbert T. Rowe, Dean of the Seminary at Duke University and one of the leading lights of the Southern Methodist Church in the first half of the twentieth century. Uncle John was better known as the Rev. Dr. John Jeter Hurt, former President of Union University and a most influential voice in the Southern Baptist Convention during that same period. Then there was Dad – the Rev. Milton N. Leininger – faithful pastor and preacher until the day he died in 1979. Foolishness? Hardly.

By the way, none of these folk would qualify for the "2,000 year old preacher" title. For that matter, nor would I. The moniker comes from a wonderful comedy routine developed over a half century ago by two of the funniest people I have ever heard, Carl Reiner and Mel Brooks. Their humor was shared in several recordings that featured Reiner as a reporter interviewing Brooks as the ancient one who is suddenly thrust into modern life.[1] He asks about the differences between back then and now. For example, what was the chief mode of transportation in the ancient world and hearing the response, "Mainly FEAR!"

I particularly remember the question about changes this man has experienced in the course of two millennia. Brooks responds in his typical exaggerated Yiddish accent, "In 2,000 years, the greatest thing mankind ever devised I think in mine humble opinion is saran wrap. You can put a sandwich in it, you can look through it, you can touch, you can put it over your face and fool around and everything. It's so good, I love it. You can put three olives in it and make a little SARAN WRAP; you can put ten sandwiches in it and make a big Saran Wrap. Whatever you want. It clings, and it sticks..."

Amidst continuous audience laughter, Reiner interrupts and asks, "You equate this with man's discovery of space?"

Brooks responds (almost sheepishly), "That was good."

The point of the whole routine is the fact that Mr. 2K-yr-old responds to our era based on the experiences formed in an era that was entirely different. The 2,000 year old preacher title comes from a parallel situation. Twenty-first century ministry is asked to interpret centuries-old texts, not only in light of their own social milieu but our own modern milieu as well. That can be quite a challenge.

As those of you in ministry know, our task is a generalist one. We have responsibilities that are wide-ranging – besides preaching, we teach, counsel, administer, provide pastoral care visiting in homes, hospitals, jails, wherever we might be needed, etc. None of us are experts in every area – we just do the best we can as God gives us guidance. The sermons published here are the result of forty years in the pulpit (not quite 2,000), years during which I concentrated my efforts on the preaching moment because this was the one time during the week that I could interact with the greatest number at the same time. My goal was always to offer something that would, in the words of the old aphorism, "comfort the afflicted and afflict the comfortable." My aim was to leave folks with something to at least think about. Only my parishioners can tell you whether I hit that mark.

Perhaps you have encountered my work in the past. My sermons and stories have been on the internet since the mid 1990's. This is my seventh book. The reason I have made the material so widely available is that, considering the "generalist" role we pastors take on, there are some whose strengths can use a boost when it comes to the task of preaching. Seminary never taught us that there is a Sunday that comes

EVERY WEEK, but such is certainly the case. If my efforts are able to help some overburdened cleric on a Saturday night after a week of hospital visits, funerals, meetings, family emergencies, etc., to prepare something meaningful for the next morning, I am glad I can pitch in.

As to choosing sermon topics, the tradition in which I was raised left it totally to the discretion of the preacher. Choose what you want. In the venerable language of the Hebrew Bible, "Everyone did what was right in his own eyes because there was no king in Israel." (Judges 21:25) There was no ecclesiastical direction or even recommendation from one week to the next. As the years went along, I came to appreciate the discipline of using the Revised Common Lectionary to choose my sermons. It delivered me from the temptation of preaching sermons that amounted week-to-week simply to 200 variations on a theme based on John 3:16. The lectionary made me deal with subjects and pericopes that I may well have avoided if left to my own devices. Thus, the current collection that is included in this book.

Feel free to use these sermons in whole or in part in your congregation. No need to give verbal credit when no one in the pews would recognize the source anyway. In print, appropriate acknowledgment is de rigueur. I recall a few years ago going online to research a particular text for some sermon starter ideas, finding some material that I found particularly helpful, reading a bit and becoming more and more impressed, only to suddenly realize IT WAS MY SERMON. This pastor had obviously found it online, preached it to his congregation, then published it online on his congregation's website with no indication that it was plagiarized word for word. Hmm. Don't do that.

As to some of the personal illustrations that you encounter, use them with a preface like, "A friend of mine tells the story of..." (And you ARE my friend if you are reading my book *grin*) or "a colleague of mine writes..." I would caution against using the material as if it were your own. I have heard more than one otherwise-distinguished preacher tell an anecdote as if it had happened to him when I had previously heard the same story from another distinguished preacher report it the same way. Well, one of them was not telling the truth!!! You never want a situation like this one – on the way home from worship in the car, the pastor's son refers to a story Dad told during his sermon that morning and asks, "Dad was that story true, or was it just preachin'?"

The one regret I have in publishing these sermons is that I cannot link them to anything that is contemporaneous with their delivery. I have always taken seriously Karl Barth's instruction to preachers about sermon preparation – do it with the Bible in one hand and a newspaper in the other. I would encourage you, as you make use of this material, to supplement it as appropriate with references to the real life situations that your listeners are encountering.

Finally, my thanks to you for allowing me the chance to participate in your ministry. In my retirement from parish work, I do not have the same opportunities that I once had, so this is a most valued extension of what I hope will someday be viewed as a useful life. God's blessings upon you as you continue in this work.

David E. Leininger
Hilton Head Island, SC

Advent 1

Mark 13:24-37

Ready!

Wait a minute. What is going on here? This is the first Sunday of Advent on the church calendar, and, more than that, it is almost Christmas. Thanksgiving is over along with "Black Friday." The shops and malls are playing "Chestnuts Roasting on an Open Fire" and "Winter Wonderland," everything is decorated to a fare thee well but we gather in church today and hear the gospel thundering about suffering and the sun being darkened, the moon without light and stars falling from the sky.

Not long ago, my wife and I joined a tourist excursion to mainland China. One day, our hosts took us to a beautiful local park where we met hundreds of Chinese locals playing board games, kicking soccer balls, doing Tai Chi exercises, folks playing music on whatever instruments they had brought. There was even a several hundred voice ad hoc choir and orchestra in the midst of a community sing. They noticed a small group of non-Asian faces so they struck up a number that they figured we could join in as well. It was "Jingle Bells." August. Ninety degrees. And we joined in with gusto:

> *Dashing through the snow,*
> *In a one-horse open sleigh.*
> *O'er the fields we go,*
> *Laughing all the way.*
> (in the public domain)

"Jingle Bells" in China — where Christmas is not a big holiday. In August. Ninety degrees. But here we are in church less than a month from the big day, and we get gloom and doom. What is going on?

Our lesson from Mark 13 is part of a chapter that is often called The Little apocalypse because it sounds so much like the language of the more famous Apocalypse that we find in the book of Revelation. As you Bible scholars know, apocalyptic literature usually comes out of scary times. In the Old Testament, for example, we find this kind of material in the book of Daniel, which comes from the era about a century and half before the birth of Christ when Antiochus Epiphanes, the Greek emperor, desecrated the temple and tried to impose pagan practices on the Jews. Jump forward a bit and we find the book of Revelation coming from the end of the first century when Christians were being persecuted because they refused to worship the Roman emperor. While this style of literature is definitely strange to us, the word apocalypse itself simply means "unveiling" or, in fact, "revelation." The style of writing wants to convey a message of hope in "code" that would not be understandable to those who are outsiders. That way the author would hope to get his or her message across without arousing the suspicion or anger of the hostile authorities.

Apocalyptic literature normally smacks of a strong and stark contrast — simply put, good versus evil. It relies on lots of symbols — numbers, colors, animals — "codes" that only the faithful would understand. It regards present dangers as passing phenomena that will lead eventually to God's ultimate victory. It is a word of hope to a persecuted faithful who, when the end is finally realized, will finally receive a godly reward. The phrase is *be ready for it.*

The Christian church has preached this theme for generations. Thus, we encounter the two mini-parables that Mark quotes. The first involves a fig tree. No curse this time as with other references in the gospels. This time, a simple observation. The disciples had asked for a sign (Mark 13:4), so Jesus offers one. Most of the trees in that part of the world are evergreen, but the olive and the fig are deciduous, losing and replacing their leaves every year. The olive tree blossoms early, so it is not a trustworthy indicator that summer is around the corner. The fig tree, however, blossoms late, so its blossoms promise that summer is almost here. This fig tree is not withered but is blossoming, a harbinger of hope.

If the first parable is about signs that should alert us, the second is a reminder to *stay* alert. A householder goes off on a journey and leaves his servants (you and me) in charge with instructions to keep watch. That was an admonition that would have resonated in that culture because they knew about instructions to Roman legionnaires who pulled guard duty — if they fell asleep on the job, they could be executed for the offense. Spiritual vigilance is important. "Therefore," in the words of Jesus, "keep awake — for you do not know when the master of the house will come, in the evening, or at midnight, or at cockcrow, or at dawn, or else he may find you asleep when he comes suddenly. And what I say to you I say to all: Keep awake."(Mark 13:37)

In some churches, the emphasis is very heavily on apocalyptic themes — the rapture of the church, the great tribulation, and the imminent return of Christ. There is the threat of being "left behind" that fueled the interest in those best-selling books and the movie that grew out of them several years ago. That is one way those who felt it was their job to tell us teens what we needed to hear to try to keep us in line — "You don't want to be caught in the back seat of the Chevy with Suzy and the windows all fogged up when the Lord returns, do you?" Gulp. The message was and is *be ready*!

Fine. But right now I would rather dial that back a notch... or two or three. To ensure against the danger of having our eyes so firmly fixed on heaven that we are no earthly good, I would encourage you to *be ready* in the here and now. Be ready for *this* life and the life to come will take care of itself.

How do we go about it? Well, I have some very good news for you. Whether you realize it or not, you have already begun... by being right here. I am absolutely convinced, after a lifetime of dealing with people at the heights, at the depths, and every place in between, that there is no better way to be ready for life out there than by spending time in here. It is here in God's house that we build the solid foundation that is crucial to surviving the winds and waves that come with the storms of life.

Ann Weems is a wonderful poet and the wife of a Presbyterian minister. Her son Todd was brutally murdered just after his twenty-first birthday. How does a mother deal with such a devastating blow? Friends tried to help and offer consolation. One was a seminary professor who called to her attention all the biblical material that seemed to be saying so much of exactly what she was feeling. Noting her prodigious poetic talent, he encouraged her to put her feelings to paper. The result is a remarkable compilation that not only helped her healing process but has helped thousands of others as well. The book is titled *Psalms of Lament* and comes from that collection in scripture where other poets have bared their souls in despair. My copy says, "To David, Through Tears — With Hope. Ann Weems." Her poetic preface, composed after her work was done, describes what she has learned:

> *In the godforsaken, obscene quicksand of life,*
> *there is a deafening alleluia*
> *rising from the souls*

of those who weep,
and of those who weep with those who weep.
If you watch, you will see
the hand of God
putting the stars back in their skies
one by one.[1]

A promise of healing and wholeness. "Through Tears — With Hope." That is the church.

We *need* one another. If you recall the story of creation from the first chapter of Genesis, you will remember the litany of "and God created this, and it was good... and God created that, and it was good, and so on." It only takes until the second chapter of Genesis for us to find something that is *not* good — "and God said, 'It is not good for man to be alone.'" No man, no woman, no boy, no girl, is an island.

This is one of the reasons I believe in the church, I encourage folks to attend, and I challenge them to join and take responsibility for what goes on. For all its flaws, for all its foibles, for all its failures, the church is God's divinely instituted way of offering people who need people the chance to find them. It offers the chance to give life meaning through involvement with others. Vaclav Havel, the first president of Czechoslovakia upon its freedom from communism (and himself a poet and playwright) once said, "The tragedy of modern man is not that he knows less and less about the meaning of his own life, but that it bothers him less and less."[2] The church cannot and will not allow such a state of blissful ignorance.

We can make a difference, you and I. The vast majority of what happens in our lives is in our hands and is very much of our own choosing. In Robert Fulghum's best-seller with that wonderful title, *It Was On Fire When I Laid Down On It*, he recounts the following conversation: he spoke with a colleague who was complaining that he had the same stuff in his lunch sack day after day. "So, who makes your lunch?" Fulghum asked.[3]

"I do," said the friend.

Up to us.

A man went for a walk in the forest and got lost. He wandered

---

1 Ann Weems, *Psalms of Lament*, (Louisville, KY: Westminster/John Knox Press, 1995), p. xvii,
2 Vaclav Havel, quoted by Martin Marty, *Context*, June 1, 1990
3 Robert Fulghum, *It Was On Fire When I Laid Down On It* (New York: Villard Books, 1990,) p. 6

around for hours trying to find his way back to town, trying one path after another, but none of them led out. Then abruptly he came across another hiker walking through the forest. He cried, "Thank God for another human being. Can you show me the way back to town?"

The other man replied, "No, I am lost too. But we can still help each other in this way — we can tell each other which path we have already tried and been disappointed in. That will help us find the one that leads out."[4]

That is exactly what Christ's church is all about. We make our way through this vale of tears, we become confused, we get lost, we search for a way out. We finally find our way with the help of others who care, others who can share with us their own disappointments, their own blind alleys, their own roads already tried.

The church. Think about how it helps you to be ready. Early on, from our first days in Sunday school, we learn that "God is great and God is good." God is big and strong and mighty, and there is nothing my God cannot do. God made this world. God made the animals and the birds. God made you and me. Even when we see news of horrible disasters like earthquakes and floods and terrorist bombings, we see miracles as little babies are found alive in the rubble, children reunited with parents after all hope had been lost. We learn that the great God of heaven can take even awful things and bring good out of them.

In the church we learn, "Your word is a lamp to my feet and a light for my path" (Psalm 119:105). The Bible — there are many good books in the world, but there are none like *the* good book. According to the American Bible Society, 87% of Americans own at least one, and the average household has three.[5] It is unrivaled as the world's all-time best-seller.

Unfortunately, most Americans are remarkably ignorant of biblical basics. One Gallup survey, for example, shows that fewer than half of our nation can name the first book of the Bible (Genesis). Only one-third knew who delivered the Sermon on the Mount (many said Billy Graham, not Jesus). One quarter could not say what we are celebrating at Easter. One New Jersey pastor made his own small effort to encourage Bible reading, posting this adage on his church sign: "A Bible that is falling apart usually belongs to a person that isn't."[6]

4 Harold Kushner, *When All You've Ever Wanted Isn't Enough*, (New York: Summit Books, 1986), p. 43
5 Smietana, Bob, *Study: Americans fond of Bible, but how many read it?*, Baptist Press, 4/25/17
6 David Gibson, Religion News Service, "Despite Being an Unequalled Best-Seller, Bible is America's Favorite Unopened Text," *The Presbyterian Outlook*, January 2001, p. 5

In the church we learn, "This little light of mine, I'm gonna let it shine." We believe, because of what we learn here, that we have a mission in this world. The gospel is good news and it demands to be shared - it deserves to be shouted from the housetops, printed on balloons, slapped on billboards, chanted at ball games, scrawled across the sky. Can't do all those things? We learn in church that one of the best ways to share the gospel is by the way we live.

Most importantly, we learn, "For God so loved the world that he gave his only begotten son, that whosoever believeth in him should not perish but have everlasting life" (John 3:16). You scholars know the name Karl Barth, probably the best-known theologian of the last century. Dr. Barth was asked near the end of his remarkable career to state the most significant truth he had come across in his lifetime of study. After a moment of thought he is reported to have answered, "Jesus loves me; this I know, for the Bible tells me so." It is in this holy place we learn that the Jesus we come to know in scripture is living and dying proof of God's love for you and for me.

Back to that trip we took to China. Our day in the Beijing park happened to be a Sunday. Normally, my wife and I would have tried to find a church on a Sunday wherever we might be, but this being China, and no one in our group being at all fluent in Chinese, we knew that our options were limited, to say the least. So God spoke to us there in that park. China and the West have been at political odds for a long time, but you would never have known that by the reception we received that day. Smiling faces, outstretched hands, folks wanting to have their photographs taken with us. All of us, in our own languages, belting out "Jingle Bells" in the summer sun.

What came to mind was that quote frequently (but inaccurately) credited to Saint Francis of Assisi: "Preach the gospel at all times; when necessary use words." Good thing that words were not necessary that day since we could never have understood each other's words anyway. The gospel that *did* come through that morning was the same one we had learned so many, many years ago. Where? In Sunday school, of course.

Jesus loves the little children,
All the children of the world.
Red and yellow, black and white,
They are precious in his sight,
Jesus loves the little children of the world.

(in the public domain)

Indeed. There will come a day... We don't know when, but it is coming. So ready or not... keep your eye out. It is going to be great!
Amen!

Stay — Tuned

Everybody loves a good story. We begin our earliest understandings through stories. The *Tortoise and the Hare*, *The Three Little Pigs*, *Jack and the Beanstalk*, *The Ugly Duckling*. We learned lessons in behavior from stories like *The Little Boy Who Cried 'Wolf'* and *Goldilocks and the Three Bears*.

The tradition of storytelling is as old as humanity itself. Ancient cultures have stories to tell younger generations about their heritage. Go to the earliest chapters of our scripture and see how our own cultural forebears answered the questions of their children and grandchildren.

"Grandpa, where did we come from?'

"Ah, my child, let me tell you a story." And what followed was the account of a man (Adam, which in Hebrew means simply *man*), a deep sleep, a disappearing rib and voilá, *woman*. Then there was the question about why there was so much wrong in this world and we hear the story about a snake in a garden. Or the question about the beautiful rainbow that appears after a storm followed by the story of Noah and the Ark — questions and answers — stories.

Jesus knew the power of stories. Much of his preaching involved parables, known better to us as stories. They taught, they challenged, they inspired, they enlightened. We learn a lot from stories.

So now we encounter a new story. At least it is new to those who were just beginning to codify what they and their friends had come to know about this incredible figure known as Jesus of Nazareth. We find it in the gospel of Mark.

As a matter of information, we really do not who Mark is. It could have been one of several folks mentioned in the New Testament — three times in the book of Acts we hear of someone called John whose surname is Mark who is associated with Peter, Paul, and Barnabas. Paul mentions a Mark as a fellow-worker. The fact that we have this material at all comes from a second-century church father named Papias who wrote,

"Mark, having become the interpreter/translator of Peter, wrote down accurately, however, not in order, all that he recalled of what was either said or done by the Lord. For he had neither heard nor followed the Lord; but later (as I said) he followed Peter, who used to adapt his instructions to the needs [of the moment or of the audience], but not with a view of making an orderly account of the Lord's sayings."[7]

So, we ultimately have no idea who wrote this gospel. Nor, for that matter, do we know for certain who actually wrote any of the gospels. We have the names listed at the top of the page, but not much else. If that bothers you and upsets your understanding of the authority and inspiration of scripture, it did me too — back in the day when I was first learning about all this, I was horrified. No longer. So, let me help you with that. Please do not think of inspired scripture as text that has somehow or other been divinely dictated, even to the extent of the names at the top of the page. Think of it as material that is so highly thought of for information, for instruction, for guidance for the faithful that the church made sure it was kept alive and disseminated through lo these many centuries. That is inspiration.

Enough about that. Scholars do tell us that Mark's gospel is the earliest of the four that we find in the New Testament. There were other writings circulating in the early church before Mark appeared — instructive materials concerning Christian behavior, and advice about dealing with those in the surrounding cultures — but none of them were designed to provide an overview of the life and ministry of Jesus. This one was breaking new ground. It begins with words that might be construed as either a title or simply a summary of what we are about to encounter. In the phrasing of the ancient King James Version of scripture in which many of us were nurtured, "The beginning of the gospel of Jesus Christ, the Son of God." More contemporary renditions say "the good news of Jesus..." (NRSV, GNT), "the wonderful story of Jesus..." (TLB), and so on. The story of Jesus. As that famous book and movie from years ago says, is *The Greatest Story Ever Told*.

By the way, one of the things of which we should be aware as we begin is this term *gospel*. It is an English translation of a Greek word, εὐαγγέλιον — *euangelion*. It is the root of our English word *evangelism*.

7 Raymond E. Brown, *An Introduction to the New Testament* (New York: Doubleday, 1997), p. 158

It means good news. In terms of literary consideration, when we read that Mark is writing "the beginning of the gospel," the word is that this is *not* simply a biography of Jesus. This is a certain literary style that has a point of view. In fact, it is a relatively new form of literature in the ancient world — biographical, yes, but with a purpose, one that wants to make a point. Which, in fact, explains why our New Testament begins with four gospels instead of just one — we have four different perspectives on Jesus' life and work. If we only had Mark, we would miss the infancy stories of Matthew and Luke — no wise men or shepherds, no Sermon on the Mount or Lord's Prayer. We would have missed out on some beautiful parables like the good samaritan and the prodigal son. Without John's beginning description of the pre-existence of the Trinity, we might have been tempted to think of Jesus as God's son in the same way that we think of ourselves as God's children. The point is that we would have missed a *lot*.

To the story… Yes, the title says it is the story of Jesus, but the first person we meet is a strange and interesting character, one whom we have come to know as John the Baptist. Actually, the gospels of Matthew, Luke and John also introduce us to John and they help us to get to know him even better. Mark simply introduces him with some Old Testament references, from the prophets Malachi (3:1) — "See, I am sending my messenger ahead of you, who will prepare your way" — and Isaiah (40:3) — "the voice of one crying out in the wilderness: 'Prepare the way of the Lord, make his paths straight.'" Mark begins with a word of hope as he harks back to the promises made generations ago that something or someone special is on the horizon.

They say that you only have one chance to make a first impression, and the first impression we get of John is *weird*. He is dressed in the garb of a wilderness man — camel's hair clothing cinched with a wide leather belt. His diet was wilderness to a fare thee well — locusts and wild honey. M-m-m. No doubt some of his appeal to those who flocked from the city to hear him was precisely his weird-ness. So be it. Whatever it takes.

Despite the unusual first impression John would have made, his preaching obviously resonated. There was a call to repentance, an invitation to baptism as a symbol of sins being washed away, and finally the promise of forgiveness.

John had a powerful impact. The account we find in Luke's gospel has folks asking what to do. "What should we do?" Sounds like an obvious question following a sermon, but one wonders. As one writer has it, "We've heard the scripture. We've heard the word preached. But nothing happens until those of us who polish the pews with our posteriors ask that question. Until we do, what we have is not a message, but a massage." Hmm.

"Repent," said John. Luke's account had the crowds asking him How? In reply he said to them, "Whoever has two coats must share with anyone who has none; and whoever has food must do likewise." Even tax collectors came to be baptized, and they asked him, "Teacher, what should we do?" He said to them, "Collect no more than the amount prescribed for you." Soldiers also asked him, "And we, what should we do?" He said to them, "Do not extort money from anyone by threats or false accusation and be satisfied with your wages" (Luke 3:10-14).

A Sunday school teacher once asked a class what was meant by the word "repentance." A little boy put up his hand and said, "It is being sorry for your sins." A little girl also raised her hand and said, "It is being sorry enough to quit."

There was a cartoon wandering around several years ago in which little George Washington is standing with an axe in his hand. Before him lying on the ground is the famous cherry tree. He has already made his smug admission that he did it — after all, he "cannot tell a lie." But his father is standing there exasperated saying, "All right, so you admit it! You always admit it! The question is, when are you going to stop doing it?"

America recently held another national election. The run-up to such events regularly has news organizations polling to get a sense of whether or not voters think the nation is going in the right direction or not. How is the economy? Good? Bad? Uncertain? What about war and peace? Are there international situations that impact us? How about our country? Are people behaving as they should or is everything a big, hot mess? Are current leaders doing a good job or do we want to get rid of what we have so we can try something new? The answer to those questions always determines the fate of candidates who reflect either a demand for "change" or a program that suggests we "stay the course."

As to personal behavior, the news regularly leers at infamous celebrities who are remarkable for nothing more than their lurid conduct. If it is any consolation, previous generations were not exempt - I remember Tallulah Bankhead once famously proclaiming that her life was "as pure as the driven slush." But that was in the days before Tabloid TV and 24/7 cable news channels. No wonder we are inclined to say we need a change.

Truth be told, systemic change starts with individual change, that good churchy word "repentance." As the old adage has it, when I point a finger at someone else, three fingers are pointing back toward me.

Psychiatrist Tom Harris, who half a century ago wrote that enormously successful book, *I'm OK, You're OK*,[8] says that there are three reasons why people change. First, people change when it is more painful to remain as they are than to change. Perhaps you are in a job that makes you miserable. You cannot imagine being in that job for the rest of your life. So, you make a change. Why? Because it is more painful to stay where you are than to change.

A second reason for change, according to Dr. Harris, is finding yourself at the point of despair. Perhaps we suddenly come to the realization that we are about to lose our marriage, our family, our health. At that point we may change. You have heard people say, "I had to reach rock bottom, before I could take hold of my life."

Harris adds a third motive for change. He calls it the "Eureka Stage." That is, some people change because they discover — much to their surprise — that there is something better that they have been missing. Of course, this is precisely the message of John's wilderness preaching. There is a richer, fuller life available to all who will receive it.

Those who heard John preach knew that they had found something that would make their lives more joyous, more purposeful, more livable. "Eureka!" This was it.

Repentance, of course, is only a first step. The next step is baptism. Think not of simply a ceremony that involves some water. Think instead of what baptism does — it introduces someone officially into the life of faith. John's instruction about baptism says we cannot handle this repentance stuff on our own — we need help. There is beautiful symbolism in the washing of water to feel clean again, whether it be from the outer grime of daily life or the inner soil of bad behavior. The symbolism helps us to grasp a greater truth.

For example, we might look together at a map, you and I, and determine the best way to get from here to New York (or anywhere else, for that matter). You might point to a spot on the paper and say, "Now here is the way to get to I-95 where we turn to the right, follow it for x-hundred miles to the Jersey Turnpike where we get on and make our way northward," and then (pointing to another spot on the paper) you might say, "And here finally is New York." Well, you and I both know that neither the intersection with I-95 nor the Jersey Turnpike nor New

8 Tom Harris, *I'm OK, You're OK* (London, *Cape*, 1970).

York are actually *on* that map, but certain symbols representing those places *are* there, symbols that are there to help show us a broader and larger reality.

Perhaps that is a good way of looking at the water of John's baptism. It is a symbol on a map to point us to the fact of God's forgiveness even though there are times when we might not quite understand all that has gone on.

But John's preaching was not done. The crowd had heard the preacher and responded, but John said, "Hold on just a minute. You have experienced something wonderful, then (just like a TV pitchman), he added, "But wait. There's more. You think this is the be-all and end-all of the power of God? My brothers and sisters, this is just the beginning. In fact, it is the beginning of the beginning. I baptized you with water. But one is coming, one who is so much more powerful than I, one who is so special that I am not worthy even to be the servant who might untie the thong of his sandals — when he baptizes you, he will wash the Holy Spirit of God over you." For a moment, the crowd thought they had already seen the whole thing. John let them know that there was more to come - not just a joyous holiday, but *more*. So, *stay tuned*.

Oh. Spoiler alert. His name is Jesus.

Amen.

Hark, The Herald... What?

This is the third Sunday of Advent on the church calendar. It's getting closer. For us who are parents and grandparents, we might have felt that way back in January, but for our little ones, they probably feel it will *never* get here. "Hark, the Herald angels sing..." Let's get to it!

In fact, we *do* get our first liturgical introduction to an angel today. A surprising one, perhaps, but an angel nonetheless. His name is John. That's right, the same John that we met in last week's lesson who gained fame of sorts by baptizing folks in the Jordan River after calling on them to repent of their sins. The John we meet today is actually the same one as last week, but this time he is not identified with his preaching and baptizing; this time he is introduced simply as a messenger, a man sent from God to introduce "the light." Jesus.

How is John an "angel?" Simple. The term "angel" is derived from the Greek word αγγελος — *angelos,* which means "messenger." *Angelos* and the Hebrew equivalent, *malak* (which also means "messenger" [the book of Malachi = My Messenger]), are the two most common terms used to describe this class of beings. In general, in texts where an angel appears, their task is to convey the message or do something on behalf of God. Since the focus of the text is on the message, the messenger is rarely described in detail. Thus, the divine emissary may or may not be some sort of supernatural being. He or she might even be dressed in a camel's hair tunic cinched with a wide leather belt.

To be sure, folks are fascinated by the whole idea of angels. Best seller lists regularly have popular titles about angels. Michael Landon starred for five years as an angel sent to earth to assist mortals in *Highway to Heaven*; CBS had a similar show which aired on Saturday nights called *Touched by an Angel*. There was that wonderful movie several years ago starring John Travolta called *Michael*, with our hero being about as *un*like our normal image of an angel as possible — he was presented as paunchy, unshaven, slovenly, and sporting wings such as might have been grafted from a giant soot-smudged pigeon. But he was sweet — over and over he said, "There is no such thing as too much sugar." Remember those?

You do not hear much preaching about angels despite the many biblical references to them. Some years ago, Billy Graham decided to do a sermon on angels and realized that he had never heard one. It prompted him to, not only preach a sermon, but write an entire book on the subject: *Angels, God's Secret Agents.*[9]

Some years ago, when the internet was just coming into its own, I decided that the church I served should have a presence on the web to reach folks who otherwise might have no contact with us at all. It was relatively easy to put up a website, and so we launched one, the first congregation to do so in Greensboro, North Carolina. It had much the same type of information as any church website has today - location, service times, events, activities, and sermons... a new one every week. It attracted a lot of attention, was written up in the newspapers, and so on. No big deal these days, but back then, something on the cutting edge. I mention that because one of the first sermons I posted had to do with angels,[10] and, to this day, that sermon has attracted more email than any of the hundreds that are currently on my website. One of the notes came from a university student who was involved in a research project on angels and, in his web search, he had come across the sermon and was writing to comment on it. Oh yes, the student was in Indonesia. Amazing!

Another was from a lady, somewhere in the US, I have no idea where. She wrote:

My fifty-year-old mother died in July from cancer and complications from cancer. Needless to say, I have been very overwhelmed with emotions, one of which was my anger with God, and why he chose my mother at this particular stage of our lives, young and starting out, growing families, etc. I could not understand his reasoning, but had no choice to accept it, although I did not truly accept it in my heart. Just recently I had an angelic experience that has put all my anger to rest.

9 Waco, TX : Word Publishing, 1975
10 Rev. Dr. David E. Lenninger, "Angels," *The Presbyterian Pulpit*, October 22, 1995. http://www.leiningers.com/angels.html

The writer went on to describe seeing a girl who appeared saying there was a ghost outside. She ran to see and what she perceived was a shadowy image, three dimensional, of her mother who looked at her, smiled and waved, and gave a big thumbs up — something she always did. In that second, the dream was over. The email continued:

> *I called my pastor in the morning and he told me of people in the Bible with angelic experiences and said that if I believe in what happened, I can feel chosen to know I had a true gift from God. I will tell you this - my anger with God has subsided. I still wish I could have my mom with me here on earth, but knowing I can't is ok with me. When I saw her, she was so much happier than I ever remembered her being. After the hardships my mom was dealt, it sure felt good seeing her so happy... I've heard of a few stories where people said they've experienced angels, but never really thought whether I believed them or not. I thought their stories were neat, but that was it. I hope you can read this with an open mind. I don't know you, but I am sharing something with you that is so special to me. Reading that you were a minister, made me feel better, but I still am a little leery. Your sermon was the closest thing I've found on the internet that related to my experience. So, I thought you must have some feelings or insight to such experiences. Please be honest, but gentle. I've been in tears most of the days since this happened, because I am elated that I got to see her again. Tears of joy to the whole experience. Thank you for your time.*

I do have some feelings or insight as to such experiences. I agree with Shakespeare who we remember saying in *Hamlet*, "There are more things in heaven and earth, Horatio, than are dreamed of in your philosophy."(*Hamlet*, 1.5 159–167)

According to regular Gallup Polls, significant numbers of Americans who believe in God also believe in angels, and indications are that more women believe than men. That surprises me a little - after all, how many men describe their wives as angels? "My wife is an angel... always up in the air harping about something." (Sorry about that; I couldn't resist — grin.)

So saying, if there is such a thing as a universal idea, one that cuts across cultures and religions, common through the centuries, it is this belief in angels. Not only do Christians, Jews, and Muslims (the monotheistic religions) have angels, but Buddhism, Hinduism, Zoroastrianism do too; winged figures appear in primitive Sumerian carvings, Egyptian tombs and Assyrian reliefs. Angels litter the metaphysical landscape from ancient times to the present.

What does the Bible say about angels? They are not only messengers, they are presented as mediators between God and us, God's heavenly entourage. Terms such as "sons of God," "holy ones," and "heavenly host" seem to focus on angels as celestial beings. As such, these variously worship God, attend God's throne, or comprise God's army. These terms are used typically in contexts emphasizing the grandeur, power, and/or mighty acts of God.

By the way, those cute cuddly little cherubs on Christmas cards do not reflect the Biblical image; after all, most every time someone encounters an angel in scripture, the first words out of the angel's mouth are *fear not*. Who would be afraid of one of those chubby little munchkins?

So, where did the angels come from? The Bible does not say other than to affirm that since only God is eternal, angels must therefore be created beings. They are not ghosts or spirits of the dead. They do not spend time trying to 'earn their wings' like the sweetly ministering Clarence in the annual Christmas movie, "It's a Wonderful Life." No place in Christian theology do we find any reference to humans becoming angels.

What do angels look like? In the Bible, the appearance of angels varies. Only cherubim and seraphim are represented with wings. Often in the Old Testament angels appear as ordinary men. Sometimes, however, their uniqueness is evident as they do things or appear in a fashion clearly non-human. The brilliant white appearance common to the New Testament angel is not a feature of the Old Testament image. So, yes, even a rough-looking wilderness preacher can fit the bill.

How about gender? Are there boy angels and girl angels? Some point to Jesus words in Mark 12:25 about there not being marriage as we understand it in heaven; instead we will, to use his words, "be like angels;" many have interpreted that as meaning that angels are sexless (which would mess John Travolta's Michael up *big* time). But then there is that passage in Genesis 6:2 which says, "the sons of God (or 'angels') saw that the daughters of men were beautiful, and they married any of them they chose." In other words, I would not bet the ranch on either position — the Bible is not clear here. And, by the way, just because the Bible is not clear, this fact has never hindered theologians from speculations — I will not go into them all here, but if you are interested, you can check that old sermon on our website for some of them.

One of the subjects with which that sermon dealt remains one of biggest questions people have regarding angels, specifically guardian angels — do we have them? Lots of folks believe so. The passage in Psalm 91 suggests *yes*: "For he will command his angels concerning you to guard you in all your ways; they will lift you up in their hands, so that you will not strike your foot against a stone." There is Jesus' comment in Matthew 18:10 (DLNT): "See that you do not look down on one of these little ones. For I tell you that their angels in heaven always see the face of my Father in heaven."

In Billy Graham's book is the story of the Reverend John G. Paton, pioneer missionary in the New Hebrides Islands. He told a thrilling tale of hostile natives surrounding his mission headquarters one night, intent on burning the Patons out and killing them. John Paton and his wife prayed all during that terror-filled night that God would deliver them. When daylight came they were amazed to see that, unaccountably, the attackers had left. Praise God from whom all blessings flow!

A year later, the chief of the tribe was converted to Jesus Christ, and Mr. Paton, remembering what had happened, asked the chief what had kept him and his men from burning down the house and killing them. The chief replied in surprise, "Who were all those men you had with you there?"

The missionary answered, "There were no men there; just my wife and I." The chief argued that they had seen many men standing guard — hundreds of big men in shining garments with drawn swords in their hands. They seemed to circle the mission station so that the natives were afraid to attack. God's angels? The chief agreed that there was no other explanation. Do you have one?

I will say this: I *do* have a problem with some stories. In my files I have one of a woman who says she was prevented from going into a certain building at a certain moment because she was held back by an unseen hand on her shoulder. She looked around but saw no one nearby. She tried again and was stopped again. Whirling around, she still saw no one.[11] But then she heard a clear voice: "It would not be wise for you to go in there just now." Hours later she learned that there was a woman

11 Eileen Elias Freeman, *Touched by Angels*, (New York: Warner Books, 1993)

murdered in the building, just after she would have entered. It could have been her — it probably would have been her, she thought. She got down on her knees and gave thanks. But the story raises a disturbing question: if she was actually saved by an angel, why did the other woman have to die? Where was *her* angel? Are angels partial to certain humans — does even God play favorites? I have never heard an answer that satisfies me.

What do you think? In the comic strip "Family Circus," Billy comes into the house all tattered and torn. He looks like he has been in a wreck, then a fight, then dragged for a mile or two by a team of runaway horses. He asked, "Do guardian angels take days off?"[12]

The biggest hazard in all this fascination with angels is that it can take people's focus off God, the God who created these ministering agents in the first place, the one who loves us and this whole world so much that God's own son Jesus of Nazareth, the babe of Bethlehem who grew into the Christ of Calvary, came to redeem us. Angels are a sign of God's interest in us, of God's desire to point us in the right direction. In the Bible, God uses angels to guide people to begin new ventures, to protect themselves, to wait, to trust. Certainly, God used John to introduce us to Jesus. There is no reason to think that God has stopped guiding people that way. My advice is to keep your eyes open for angels of all kinds. Do not confine yourself to wings and halos. Just remember that, biblically, the word we translate as *angel* is just as correctly translated *messenger*.

One messenger might be your conscience. "Ah, ah, ah." "Watch it." "Careful." Listen for that inner voice that keeps you from straying from the right path. An angel.

A second might be found in your dreams. This has great biblical precedent — In the Old Testament, Abimelech, Jacob, Laban, Joseph, the Egyptian Pharaoh, Gideon, and Solomon. In the New Testament, Joseph, the wise men, and the wife of Pontius Pilate, to name a few. Analyze your dreams and their symbols (if you remember them), to see what is being said to you — an angel.

Third, look for angels in the people around you every day. Years ago, I was in the process of wrestling with God in discerning where it was my ministry would take me next. I was convinced it was a church in Kansas. One morning, as Christie and I were walking, she said to me, "I don't know how you feel called to Kansas, but I feel called to North Carolina (where another church was asking me to serve). She had never said anything like that to me before — ever — an angel. And yes, we ended up in North Carolina.

Angels... A pastor went to visit a newly-married couple in his

12 *The Pastor's Story File*, Oct. 1991, 5

congregation. He knocked on the front door. A sweet voice from within called, "Is that you, angel?"

The minister replied, "No, but I'm from the same department."

Angels. No, we do not begin to have all the details available to us. But if you are interested in angels, be glad - it is a sign of a healthy hunger for the answers to the great mysteries. Listen for God's messengers and messages, even from a wild-looking character from out in the desert who is the *last* one we would ever imagine at this time of year when we raise our voices with "Hark, the herald angels sing." Remember, "There are more things in heaven and earth, Horatio, than are dreamed of..." *Hamlet* (1.5 167-168) Angels.

Amen!

Mary's Complaint

I suppose you have had the chance to watch at least a little television during these busy days before Christmas. Have you noticed that the news programs are carrying more stories about unfortunate people these days... people who have lost their homes, people who are facing debilitating disease, people who seem to have had their whole world fall in on them? Have you noticed that? I understand why: somehow the plight of desperate folks seems all the more desperate in the midst of what should be a season of unbounded joy. And we would expect them to echo the lament of the psalmist: "O Lord God of hosts, how long will you be angry with your people's prayers? You have fed them with the bread of tears, and given them tears to drink in full measure. You make us the scorn of our neighbors; our enemies laugh among themselves. Restore us, O God of hosts; let your face shine, that we may be saved." (Psalm 80:4-7)

But I have noticed something else. Those desperate folks, for the most part, do not lament or complain very much. In spite of all they would have every reason to complain about, they don't... at least not on camera... stiff upper lip and all that. And then we think about it and become a little embarrassed about all the complaining that WE do - how much money we have to spend, how little time we have to get things done, and so on. We have every right to be embarrassed.

I think back to another situation in which someone had all the reason in the world to complain... but did not. Take those television news cameras back two thousand years to the little town of Nazareth in Galilee. *There* is a truly heart rending story... someone with as much ground for complaint as anyone of us will ever see. You already know her name... *Mary*.

We do not know how old she was, but tradition has it that she was just a teenager, perhaps fifteen or sixteen, or even younger. She had grown up in a religious home, and despite the fact that, as a female she was barred from the formal training of the synagogue, she had developed a special relationship with her God.

She was preparing to enter a new phase of life. It had been arranged for her to marry a local carpenter, a man named Joseph. That is the way marriages are put together in the Middle East, back then as well as now — it is believed that something as important as marriage should not be left to the whims of the heart. The engagement had been agreed to and the period of betrothal had begun.

Now... catastrophe. She was pregnant. An angel had appeared to her and said that she would bear a son. True, the angel had said wonderful things to her: this was happening because she had found favor with God; the child would be great and be called the Son of the Most High; he would grow up to become a king... wonderful things. She had questioned the situation because she knew well enough where babies come from. She had asked, "How can this be, since I am a virgin?" The angel told her not to worry: God would father the child in a supernatural way. And then the angel left.

Catastrophe... an unwed mother... and through no fault of her own. In our own day, becoming pregnant while unmarried carries a tremendous toll (grounds for complaint, to be sure), but two-thousand years ago, it could be even worse. Joseph could have gotten rid of Mary by announcing to the world her crime against him and having her killed! That was legal. Or, as he decided to do, Joseph could quietly call the whole thing off and avoid the public scandal. At any rate, Mary's life was ruined.

She surely had grounds for complaint. Here was a young girl on the brink of an exciting new life, and now this. "Greetings, favored one." Favored? What kind of favor is this? She had every right to complain, but her complaint was strange: "My soul magnifies the Lord." (Luke 1:46) Some complaint!

Of course, as time went along, she had more grounds for complaint. Some months later, she and her intended husband (who, as we know from a thousand Sunday school lessons, decided *not* to terminate their relationship) had to travel the eighty miles from Nazareth down to Bethlehem to register for the Roman census. They were liable for the imperial tax and had to register just as every other citizen under the Caesar's control... each in the city of their ancestry. Since she and Joseph were both counted as descendants of King David, they had to travel to the ancestral home: Bethlehem.

Mary surely could have complained about that. Eighty miles of travel in days when the only transportation for a poor family was in donkey caravans would be difficult enough under any circumstances... but exceedingly pregnant as well? Grounds for complaint, no question. Here was this "favored" young woman being forced to travel a difficult route under the most trying of circumstances. "Favored," indeed! She could complain, but all we hear was her saying "...let it be with me according to your word." (Luke 1:38) Strange complaint!

Mary's situation did not improve much when she and Joseph arrived in Bethlehem. This "favored" young woman who was about to give birth to the successor to David's throne might have expected, if not palatial, at least decent accommodations for the event, and if this is the family town, some relatives would certainly have a place for them. A bit of privacy, perhaps? Of course. With the animals? Well, at least they were out from under the stars. Thank heaven for small favors. Small, indeed. Not exactly in the "favored one" category. Again, Mary had every cause to complain. But what does her complaint sound like? Consider what she said to her cousin Elizabeth when the two of them met prior to the births of their sons: "Surely, from now on all generations will call me blessed; for the mighty one has done great things for me, and holy is his name." (Luke 1:48-49) A strange complaint indeed!

Then, of course, there was the birth itself. I suppose any of us would like to know that we have been "favored" by God, and that we have been selected for some signal service. But there are some types of service, quite honestly, with which we would just as soon see someone else "favored," particularly service that involves a great deal of pain. I cannot speak from first-hand knowledge, but I hear there are *no* pains to compare with those of childbirth. Now, here was a "favored" young woman; at least she might expect to be offered an opportunity for service that might not involve anguish. But no. She was granted the dubious blessing of undergoing surpassing agony as the mark of just how "favored" she really was. Mary's complaint? "His mercy is for those who fear him." (Luke 1:50) A strange way to complain.

If you have been to a hospital maternity ward recently, you are aware that visitors are kept to a minimum. After all, childbirth is a rigorous ordeal; mother and child need the chance to get their strength before being expected to do a "show and tell." A little peace and quiet, please. A young girl as "favored" as Mary might at least have been able to expect a degree of privacy after what she had gone through. After all, she had just given birth in a strange city, in abysmal surroundings, apparently without the help of a sympathetic mother or midwife, just the company of a husband who was probably more nervous than herself, and forced to use a feeding trough as a cradle for her new son. At least she might have counted on her "favored" status to guarantee her a bit of rest and privacy. But she got not even that.

Soon after the birth, some local shepherds came... to gawk. They came with a story about some angels appearing to them on the hillside outside of town telling of the birth of the one who would be the Messiah. Well, that certainly jibed with what Gabriel had announced to her nine months before. But would it not have been possible for the angels to spread the word in another day or two? After all, she *was* "favored," wasn't she? But it was not to be. Mary surely had grounds for complaint. She said, "[God] has shown strength with his arm..." (Luke 1:51) Another strange way to complain.

Somehow, one might expect that, with all Mary had been expected to endure, there would come a time when something might have been expected to go right for her. At least once the anguish of having to tell her husband-to-be that she was going to have a baby that was not his, the difficulty of a lengthy trip just before the due date, the problem of awful accommodations, the pains of the birth itself, and the lack of privacy after it was all over, Mary might have figured she had the right to *expect* that things would begin to start going her way. After all, how much "favored" status should one person be expected to endure?

But there was more to come. Word came to Mary and Joseph that King Herod had gotten wind of the fact that there was a pretender to his throne recently born in Bethlehem, and jealous of his own power as he was, Herod wanted to make certain that no one would be able to claim his place. Information had it that the king was sending troops to Bethlehem with orders to murder every baby boy under the age of two that they found. Time for another trip... this time even longer... to Egypt. They remained in Egypt as expatriates until Herod finally died. Mary surely could have complained. She had every right. But her words were, "[God] has brought down the powerful from their thrones and lifted up the lowly" (Luke 1:52). A strange way to complain.

Finally, of course, Mary and Joseph and Jesus *did* get to return to Israel. Apparently, they had planned to go back to Bethlehem, but the political situation was such that it might have been dangerous. So they went back up north to Galilee and settled down again in Nazareth. It had been a most difficult couple of years for Mary. There was not much about her life that she would have been able to celebrate. Actually, it had been one near-disaster after another. For one as "favored" as the angel had said she was, the "favor" was strange indeed. At least she might have been able to expect that she would now be able to settle down to a life of ease. After all, this son she had borne was to be the king, was he not? But no, Mary would find no particular ease. Hers would be a normal life with all the worries about raising children, keeping a home and putting food on the table that any wife might have. She could have complained, I suppose, but her words do not sound like a complaint: "[God] has filled the hungry with good things and sent the rich away empty" (Luke 1:53). Some complaint!

Maybe Mary did not know how to complain... but I doubt it. She complained later on when Jesus began his ministry. She and her other children thought he had lost his mind, and they tried to get him to stop and come home. Of course, he did not... and the rest of the story we know. No, Mary knew how to complain. She was normal; she was a human being like anyone else with all the natural tendencies to gripe and moan like any of us.

But something kept her from it. She had heard from the angel that she was "favored," and she believed it. She knew enough about what being chosen meant simply by looking at her nation's history. The Jews were God's chosen people... but chosen for what? A life of ease? A life without pain? A life with no problems? Hardly. This "chosen people" of hers had been chosen for service; it was to be a nation who would minister to the needs of a world lost in the darkness without the light of the God of heaven. She knew that to be chosen of God sometimes means both a crown of joy and a cross of sorrow. She had heard that she was "favored," and, in faith, she was willing to accept whatever that favor meant.

Interesting, is it not, how many others in history have been "favored" of God in being given some tremendous task to do. Paul was "favored," favored with the task of sharing the Gospel with the Gentiles, and ended up being able to write that "I have learned to be content in whatever situation I find myself" (Philippians 4:11 ISV). He wrote that from a prison cell. The martyrs to the faith thought of themselves as "favored." One named Polycarp said as he was about to be burned ALIVE, "Father, I bless you for counting me worthy of this day and hour." A list like that could go on and on... everyone with grounds for complaint but none willing to do so. "Favored."

How many of us would count ourselves as "favored?" Not us. We are not in the class of a Mary, a Paul, or a Polycarp. We do not think of ourselves as heroes of the faith. And it is just as well. We would rather someone else have all that "favor" considering what it might entail. And way down deep, we would rather hang on to the right to complain. Too bad, because God does not seem to make that much use of complainers.

No, we do not have as much to complain about as Mary. We do not even have as much to complain about as those folks whose stories we see on the evening news... but we do it anyway. Shame on us.

If anyone had cause for complaint it was Mary. Listen and learn from her: "My soul magnifies the Lord, and my spirit rejoices in God my Savior, for he has looked with favor on the lowliness of his servant. Surely, from now on all generations will call me blessed; for the Mighty One has done great things for me, and holy is his name." (Luke 1: 46-49) Mary's remarkable complaint.

Amen.

Nativity Of Our Lord

Luke 2:1-20

God Bless Santa!

Several years ago, when Donald Trump was running for the US Presidency, he wanted to convince evangelical voters that he was one of them, so he let it be known that he was a Christian, born and raised Presbyterian even. That was a bit of a surprise to us Presbyterians, but no matter. Reporters pressed him on that and asked which he preferred, the Old Testament or the New. He said he liked them both. They asked him what was his favorite Bible verse; he said he didn't have a favorite, he liked them all. Uh-huh.

Well, most of us *do* have a favorite or two, and I would be willing to bet (although raised as a Presbyterian, I was taught early on that such would be frowned upon) that many would choose John 3:16. "For God so loved the world, that he gave his only begotten Son, that whosoever believeth in him should not perish, but have everlasting life." An unusual text for this time of year, eh? Not really. Stay with me (John 3:16).

Admittedly, things can be confusing right now. You are familiar with the cartoon, "Family Circus." At Christmas time, Big Sister comes to P. J. and says, "Want me to tell you a story, P. J.? Jesus was born just in time for Christmas up at the North Pole surrounded by eight tiny reindeer and the Virgin Mary. Then Santa Claus showed up with lots of toys and stuff and some swaddling clothes, the Three Wise Men and the elves all sang carols, while the Little Drummer Boy and Scrooge helped Joseph trim the tree. In the meantime, Frosty the Snowman saw the star...".[13]

Hmm. As we say, confusing. It is even confusing in the church — congregations regularly wrestle with how to go about the celebration. We look at the calendar and see that December 25th has not come yet — but there is still the temptation to jump right over Advent and directly to Christmas in our music and worship. The mall does it; why not us? Then there are the obligatory annual reminders that "Jesus is the Reason for the Season," and to "Keep Christ in Christmas," despite the fact that

13 Bill Keane, "Family Circus," *King Features Syndicate*Quoted by Ross W. Mars, "God Was Christ", *Church Management: The Clergy Journal*, Nov/Dec/1990, ibid p. 44..

we know he has never left it. We come into church on a Sunday and beat ourselves up about excessive spending, excessive partying, excessive scurrying, excessive *excesses*, then go out and repeat the process all over again.

The reason for all the confusion is that we are celebrating two holidays at this time of year, not one. They are related — both are called Christmas — but they are very different; one is sacred, the other, as young Marvin would ruefully note, is secular.

If it is any comfort, the confusion goes way, way back. If you look up the origins of Christmas in the encyclopedia, you will find material like this:

> *The reason why Christmas came to be celebrated on December 25 remains uncertain, but most probably the reason is that early Christians wished the date to coincide with the pagan Roman festival marking the "birthday of the unconquered sun" (natalis solis invicti); this festival celebrated the winter solstice, when the days again begin to lengthen and the sun begins to climb higher in the sky. The traditional customs connected with Christmas have accordingly developed from several sources as a result of the coincidence of the celebration of the birth of Christ with the pagan agricultural and solar observances at midwinter. In the Roman world the Saturnalia (December 17) was a time of merrymaking and exchange of gifts. December 25 was also regarded as the birth date of the Persian mystery god Mithra, the Sun of Righteousness. On the Roman New Year (January 1), houses were decorated with greenery and lights, and gifts were given to children and the poor.[14]*

Okay. You have probably heard all that before, or at least variations of it. But, to be accurate, the choice of December 25 as the date to celebrate the holy birth is not as mysterious as some would have us believe. You see, there is another festival which the church has observed for centuries (and even before any celebration of Christmas) called the Feast of the Annunciation. It is observed on March 25 and commemorates the angel Gabriel's visit to Jesus' mother: "Do not be afraid, Mary, you have found favor with God. And now, you will conceive in your womb and bear a son, and you will name him Jesus." (Luke 1:30-31). Do the math. Nine

14 Hans J, Hilderbrand, "Christmas" *Encyclopaedia Britannica*, © 1994-1998

months from March 25 is December 25. Voilá! Christmas. Is that really the date of Jesus' birth? Probably not, but at least you can see where it came from — it is *more* than simply a "Christianizing" of Saturnalia.

Yes, the celebration became a big deal, despite the fact that the church insisted then (as it does now), that the *really* big deal is Easter. By the fifth century, the Festival of the Nativity had taken on such importance in the Christian world that it signaled the beginning of the liturgical year. This continued up until the eleventh century when the period of Advent was added to the Christmas cycle and the first Sunday in Advent from then on became the start of the new liturgical year, a practice which, as you know, continues to this day.[15]

Along the way, Christian beliefs combined with existing pagan feasts and winter rituals to create many of the long-standing traditions of Christmas celebrations which we continue to observe. Christmas trees, decorations, parties, gift giving, and so on. Mistletoe? Ancient Europeans believed that the mistletoe plant held magical powers to give life and fertility, to bring about peace, and to protect against disease. Northern Europeans associated the plant with the Norse goddess of love, Freya, and developed the custom of kissing underneath mistletoe branches. We Christians stole the practice, and I, for one, am forever grateful!

Of course, the celebrations can become excessive. For a brief time during the seventeenth century, the Puritans banned Christmas in England and in some English colonies in North America because they felt it had become a season best known for gambling, flamboyant public behavior, and overindulgence in food and drink. Sound familiar?

What it all amounts to is this: confusion. Yes, as people of faith at Christmas we celebrate God's incomparable gift of Jesus, the one who bridges the gap between earth and heaven, our Redeemer, our Savior. But as products of our culture, we also celebrate the secular appurtenances that have grown up around the festival. Both are called Christmas, but they are very different. One holiday has fir trees, tinsel and trappings, and these days, secular Christmas begins with TV commercials as soon as the back-to-school specials are done in September. The other holiday has a humble birth, lowly shepherds, heavenly angels, God in human flesh, and begins on Christmas Eve. Two Christmas celebrations. Very different, but I would insist that they need not be mutually exclusive. If we can learn to separate them, then we might actually come to enjoy both. They can complement one another rather than compete with one

15 "Origins of the Religious Festival," https://www.chin.gc.ca/christmas/presentn.htm

another.

Now, with that in mind, hear again this favorite scripture text: "For God so loved the world, that he gave his only begotten Son, that whosoever believeth in him should not perish, but have everlasting life." (John 3:16) For God so loved the world that he gave... What could be more "Christmassy" than giving? Christmas is the one time of the year when our thoughts tend more toward giving than to getting. Even the most selfish among us find our thoughts turned toward others. We go out of our way to consider family and friends. We even do things for people we normally forget: food baskets for the poor, toys for tots, and so on. You remember what happened to Ebenezer Scrooge in *A Christmas Carol* — after being the stingiest man in all of literature, because of Christmas, he changes. And finally, he vows near the end of the story to "honor Christmas in my heart and try to keep it all the year."

In my files is a brief note recalling a television show that was on years ago, "Doogie Howser, MD." Remember that one? I never bothered to watch very often because the premise of a teenage physician weighing matters of life and death equally with the trials and tribulations of puberty was a bit too silly for me. So saying, I do recall seeing an episode around this time of year which had Doogie spending half of the show trying to get out of working on Christmas Eve so he could go to a party, and the other half of the show repenting of the deception he had employed to accomplish that questionable end. At the end of the program, Doogie sat down in front of his personal computer and made an entry into his electronic journal. He wrote, "Getting is good — Giving is better. Once you understand that, it's always Christmas." Hear, hear!

Christmas text: "For God so loved the world that he *gave*..."

And who is the personification of giving in our culture? Our kids know if we don't — Santa Claus. Christian pulpits occasionally object to putting too much emphasis on Saint Nick, and there is no question that it happens. But if Jesus has to share these celebrations with anyone, I am glad it is Santa because that jolly old elf with the strange wardrobe and the desperate need of a haircut makes the idea of giving come alive in ways that no pulpit ever has. The sacred and the secular meet. God bless Santa!

At this time of year, we hear again that famous editorial that appeared in the *New York Sun* in 1897 in response to a little girl's letter. She wrote, "Dear Editor: I am eight years old. Some of my little friends say there is no Santa Claus. Papa says, 'If you see it in *The Sun* it's so.' Please tell me the truth — is there a Santa Claus?" and the letter was signed,

"Virginia O'Hanlon."

The response was a classic. It read in part, "Virginia, your little friends are wrong. They have been affected by the skepticism of a skeptical age. They do not believe except what they see. They think that nothing can be which is not comprehensible by their little minds. All minds, Virginia, whether they be men's or children's, are little. In this great universe of ours, man is a mere insect, an ant, in his intellect, as compared with the boundless world about him, as measured by the intelligence capable of grasping the whole of truth and knowledge.

"Yes, Virginia, there is a Santa Claus. He exists as certainly as love and generosity and devotion exist... How dreary would be the world if there were no Santa Claus! It would be as dreary as if there were no Virginias...

"No Santa Claus! Thank God he lives, and he lives forever. A thousand years from now, Virginia... no, ten times ten thousand years from now, he will continue to make glad the heart of childhood."[16]

It was a beautiful response to a little girl's question. Of course, as Virginia grew older, she began to conceive of Santa Claus in a different way than when she was eight years old. We all do. As Paul wrote, "When I became a man, I put childish ways behind me" (1 Cornthians 13:11). But the image of that broad, happy face "and a little round belly that shook when he laughed like a bowl full of jelly" continue to bring us joy no matter how old we become. It is an image of giving, of generosity, of unselfishness, of love, that is without parallel in all of mythology. That is why I say, "God bless Santa!"

Yes, there is a parallel between the myth and the fact. It cannot be pressed too far, but this spirit of giving that we celebrate in Santa Claus finds its root in the other celebration, the *real* Christmas story. It was totally generous, totally unselfish, totally loving for God to give us Jesus...our Savior. As scripture has it, "But when the fullness of time had come, God sent his Son, born of a woman, born under the law, in order to redeem those who were under the law, so that we might receive adoption as children." (Galatians 4:4-5). Children do not have to worry about "better watch out/better not cry," because he seems to come to us most especially at the point of our tears. Children need not concern ourselves that "He's gonna find out who's naughty and nice," because he already knows all the things that make us fail to live up to even old Scrooge's promise about honoring Christmas all the year. He comes to us and invites us to accept the gift he offers. The Christmas verse is,

16 Francis P. Church, Is There a Santa Claus? *New York Sun*, September 21, 1897

"For God so loved the world that he *gave* his only begotten Son, that whosoever believeth in him should not perish, but have everlasting life (John 3:16)."

Giving *is* what Christmas is all about. God has given us a wonderful gift. Jesus. Celebrate the gift. And celebrate the other Christmas as well, the one that features Santa, our culture's personification of giving — sitting there in the center of the mall with kids on his lap, standing on a street corner ringing a bell beside a kettle, going "Ho, Ho, Ho" as he rides his sleigh into the night sky of your TV screen — because Santa is about giving too. God bless Santa.

Which holiday are you going to celebrate this year? Both, I hope. Both are wonderful. If you are like me, before December 24, you went to the parties, sent Christmas cards, decorated the house, and probably spent more money than you had planned. But now that the holy night has arrived, you leave the noisy party and join the commemoration of something beyond imagining - the incarnation, the coming of the Lord of all the universe in human flesh in the person of the Babe of Bethlehem. Amazing! "For God so loved the world that he gave his only begotten Son, that whosoever believeth in him should not perish but have everlasting life." No wonder it is a favorite verse of many Christians. Enjoy the celebrations. Enjoy both Christmases. And God bless us everyone!

Amen!

Simeon (A Monologue)

I am old and ready to die. To be truthful, I have been ready to die for years, but right now, I feel ready as I have never been before. You see, earlier today, in the temple in Jerusalem, I met a young couple who had come with their young son for the ritual of purification, and I knew when I saw them that a promise which God had made to me had been fulfilled. Now I am ready to die.

I suppose I should explain. Perhaps you know me; perhaps you don't. My name is Simeon. I am a rabbi, a member of the Sanhedrin, one of the seventy men charged with the oversight of Jewish faith throughout the world. We are responsible for the purity of our religion. We are the ones to whom the people look for guidance concerning true and false teachers; we are the ones ordained by God to keep the faith in the face of a hostile and unbelieving world. It is a grave task, but one which every one of us is pleased and honored to undertake.

To be sure, there are great varieties of opinion among the members of the Sanhedrin. Some are Sadducees... including the high priest. They are the most conservative of us. They go so far as to say that nothing matters at all except what is written in the Torah. For them, any further explanation is the work of man, not of God, and as such must be totally ignored when it might deal with a subject that Moses did not discuss. That is why the Sadducees do not believe in the resurrection of the dead — Moses did not talk about it, so therefore, it must not be true. The Sadducees, because the high priest is a Sadducee, are the real power among us.

I myself would be classed with the Pharisees. We too hold to the importance of the Torah, but we believe that God made no effort to give all information about everything that would ever happen to Moses. We believe that God is continually revealing himself / the world to us, and that continuing revelation needs interpretation. The people of this day need to know what their heavenly Father requires of them in this day.

If people hear the law read in the temple or their synagogues, they need to be able to understand its relevance in the here and now. Those who would live righteous lives need to know that sort of thing. We believe that the law is a living, breathing, vital gift from God — a way to help us order our lives so that we might be pleasing. Some have accused us of taking liberties with the word of God in making the interpretations we do, but I disagree. Interpretations have to be made or else people will flounder in a sea of uncertainty.

But really, I get away from my story here. Although there are differences in theology among us, *all* Jews share one thing in common: a hope for a deliverer... the Messiah. Every member of the Sanhedrin, every Jewish man and woman in Jerusalem, everyone who fears God anywhere in the world is looking for the coming of the one whom God will use to unite the people under one banner. But so saying, we even have differences among ourselves about the Messiah.

There are some who are looking for a military leader, one who will break the rod of our oppressors. To be sure, we have been oppressed. To be clear about it, we have had many in the past on whom we looked as Messiah. The name simply means "Anointed One," and the kings of our history fell into that category — they were anointed when they ascended the throne. The greatest of all of them was our father, David. It was he who united us as a nation to stand against our ancient enemies and led us to victory after victory in battles against them. Ever since David, we have looked for others who could do what he did.

As time went along, we were blessed with other good and successful kings, although none quite measured up in comparison to David. Our dream never came true.

Most assuredly, there are some... the Zealots, who still hold on to that dream in spite of the fact that no one has sat on David's throne for centuries. They say that a leader will one day rise up, overthrow all the foreign powers within our borders, and be a new David. They say it is just a matter of time.

But there are some of us who have come to the conclusion that God's plan for the people no longer involves military might and conquest. We have begun to look for a different kind of Messiah, one who will deliver us, not just in this life, but through all the ages of eternity. Some of my brethren might be disappointed at such a Messiah — they would rather have a commander of armies. But I am becoming more and more convinced that this will not be the case.

Actually, I should say I have become convinced and that is why this day has been so special to me. I have met that new Messiah, and indeed I have held him in my arms.

Perhaps I should say something about myself here. I can say honestly that throughout my years, I have done everything I could to live a life that is pleasing to God. As a boy, I went to the synagogue schools and excelled in my lessons. I grew to love God's law and was glad to be encouraged to become a rabbi.

Even though my parents had arranged a marriage for me, I almost felt that the only true marriage I could have would be to the Torah. However, I felt a certain sense of obligation and was joined to my wife as our families had planned. I can say now that I am grateful that such an arrangement was made because my wife Sarah has proven to be a most faithful and supportive spouse. She gave me a son, Gamaliel, who I can proudly say has followed in my footsteps and become a teacher of the law. I have tried to be a good husband and father.

But as important to me as my family relationship was and is, even more important has been my relationship with my creator. I have always been scrupulous in my observance of God's commands. I never fail to keep the sabbath; I tithe of all that I have; I make the proper sacrifices. I come here to the temple daily for prayer. I am loyal to many things: to my family, to my work, to my students. But I am first and most importantly loyal to my God.

Perhaps that is why God revealed to me that I would someday see the Messiah. I remember it well: I was in the temple for prayer in the afternoon as is my custom. I was wrestling with the Lord over this question of deliverance for Israel. I was asking for guidance for the discussions I had been having with some of my synagogue students concerning the salvation of the nation. I was going over all the arguments for and against a coming military chieftain and searching in my prayers for an answer. When suddenly, it was as if a voice was speaking inside me... a voice the like of which I had never heard. And it said to me, "Simeon, fear not, for I am the Lord, the God whom you serve. You have been faithful to me and I shall be faithful to you. A Messiah *will* come, and you shall not come to the end of your days until you have seen him." I was dumbfounded. I wanted to ask more about this Messiah but I could not. The answer was not really there... about whether he would be a military leader or not... but it made no difference. A Messiah *would come*, and he would come in my lifetime.

I recall thinking as I made my way home whether or not I should tell my students about the strange event. But I finally decided that I would keep it to myself. After all, if God wanted the information revealed to them, God would have told me. So, I kept it to myself.

Until now. You see, now I can say something about it, because now the Messiah has come. I know he has come. I met him. I held him in my arms... this very day. He was just a tiny baby, but somehow, God revealed to me that this baby was the one. He would be the deliverer of Israel, and more than that, he would be the deliverer of the entire world.

I had come into the temple courts to pray. As I walked through the Court of Women on my way into the Court of Israel, my eye was struck by a couple, a young woman and an older man, evidently her husband, walking together. A child, an infant really, was in the mother's arms. Something impelled me to walk over to them, I'm not sure what. But I did. I went over and spoke to them. They told me that they were from Nazareth in Galilee but they had come down to Jerusalem for the ritual purification as required by the Torah. I smiled at the baby... a most handsome child — jet black hair, deep brown eyes. All babies are beautiful. As I stood there admiring him, his parents went on to tell me that they had named him Jesus, a not uncommon name in our day. The name meant "salvation" and many a proud parent had chosen the name for their firstborn in hopes that *he* might be the one chosen to deliver the nation. But as I stood there listening to them, that voice I had heard once before inside of me came back and said "This is he of whom I spoke. He will save his people... from their sins."

Once again, I was dumbfounded. I wanted to call to the voice and ask for more. "...from their sins?" What about from Rome? But I couldn't speak for a moment... and the voice was gone.

With my eyes and hands, I let the mother know that I would like to take the child in my arms. She smiled at me and handed him to me. I looked down into those brown eyes and felt his little arms as they waved back and forth. And suddenly, I remembered why I had come to the temple in the first place... to pray. And I felt like praying... *right there*. I lifted up my eyes to heaven and prayed the most joyful prayer I ever had. "Master, now you are dismissing your servant in peace, according to your word; for my eyes have seen your salvation, which you have prepared in the presence of all peoples, a light for revelation to the Gentiles and for glory to your people Israel." (Luke 2:29-32) And then I stood there for a moment, my eyes still fixed on heaven. It was as if I as a bond-slave had just been told by my owner that I was to be a free man from henceforth. I was ready to be freed. Indeed, I was ready to die and meet my God face to face.

Then I looked back down toward the child and finally to his parents. They were staring at me, not knowing quite what to make of what I had said. I smiled gently at them. I wanted to let them know that I was not just some senile old man with no idea of what he was saying. I tried to reassure them with a blessing upon them and their son. Then I handed the baby back to his mother.

As she took him from me, I felt compelled to say something further. I would have loved to have let my conversation end with the blessing, but that strange something inside me led me to share my feelings: Joy, to be sure, but mixed with a sense of disquiet. I looked at the young woman and said, "This child is destined for the falling and the rising of many in Israel." Even though God had not specifically revealed it to me, I knew that this child would be a different kind of Messiah than many were expecting. He would lead gently, not with any army; He would teach rather than demand; he would heal rather than destroy. There would be many of our countrymen who would not be able to abide that. Though his aim might be to bring peace, He would actually bring a sword. I knew too that that young mother would someday be hurt more deeply than anyone can imagine... not by her son, but by what others would do to her son. Please understand me: I am not making myself out to be a soothsayer or a fortuneteller; I could not possibly know the details of this young family's future life. But somehow, I know that their path will not be strewn with roses. I felt led to warn them.

I am not sure if they understood, because right at that moment, the prophetess Anna came up to us, the same Anna who has been living and worshiping in the temple for lo these many years since the death of her husband. Suddenly, she too began saying the same things I had about this child being the salvation of Israel. If the boy's parents had had any doubts about the truth of what I had said before, Anna most certainly removed them. As the Torah says, two witnesses are needed to confirm a report, and now two witnesses had spoken.

Within a moment, the young family had made its way out of the temple precincts and I was left alone again to gather my thoughts. They surely did need gathering. I had wanted to say more to them, but it's probably just as well that there was no opportunity — I don't know what I would have said. So, I made my way into the inner court and began my prayers... prayers of thanksgiving like none had ever been given before. I was thankful for what I had seen, thankful that I had seen it, and thankful for a God who was faithful to eternal promises. My prayers complete, I made my way out here... to the quiet of the countryside... to contemplate... to wonder... perhaps to die.

I am ready. I have lived a long and full life. I have raised a fine son who will carry on after me. I am most certainly at peace with my God. How could I be otherwise when God has honored me this way? I am ready.

It is strange, now that I think on it. As I mentioned, I am a Pharisee, we do believe in the resurrection of the dead. I recall one of the questions that somehow gets repeated among us almost every time the subject of resurrection comes up: what actually happens when we finally meet Adonai face to face? Of course, we firmly believe there will be a judgment, but what will be judged? Some of us have speculated that our Creator will ask us one question that will show just where we stand; we will be asked, "Where have you looked for salvation?" An interesting question. For some, the answer will be, "In the power of the Roman Caesar;" for others, "in one who could overthrow the Roman Caesar;" for still others, the answer might be, "in the Torah." Until today, that last answer might have been the one I would have given, but no longer. Now I will answer, "My salvation is in the Lord God of heaven who is faithful to the promise and in the child now sent to redeem the world."

I am reminded of the prophet Isaiah as he rhapsodized on the accession of a king so many centuries ago, "For unto us a child is born, unto us a son is given...." (Isaiah 9:6 KJV) Now, here it is 700 years later, and I feel like saying the same thing. This baby, this child, this son, this Jesus has come. And now, Simeon is ready to die. Because in him, and in him *alone*, we have our salvation.

Amen.

And The Word Became Flesh

Christmas is such a marvelous time of the year... music, laughter, celebration... especially for children. We see the joy on their faces as they go through the season — watching trees being gaily decorated, seeing all the toys in the stores, anticipating the annual visit of Santa Claus — it's a time of real excitement... for both the young and the young at heart.

To be sure, it is a particularly exciting time for Christians. After all, the culmination of the season is the celebration of the birth of the Savior; of the God in Heaven taking on human form; as John's Gospel says, of the Word becoming flesh and living among us. Someone has said that the five most important words in the Bible are these: "And the Word became flesh." (John 1:14) Without them, we have no life of Jesus, no Sermon on the Mount, no atoning death, no victory in resurrection, no way we can know God as God wishes to be known.

"And the Word became flesh." There is every reason for excitement in that. But there is reason for a great deal of wonder along with the excitement, a wonder that should provoke us to some deep and reverent thought at Christmas time. To be honest, the next few minutes are more Bible study than sermon, so bear with me a bit because I don't want to lose you.

First, we need to look at the situation in which John was writing. It was probably around the end of the first century. There were Jews in the church, of course, since Judaism was the soil from which Christianity grew — Jesus himself was obviously a Jew. But there were now Greeks as well, lots and lots of Greeks from all over the known world. How can John address both groups and have both understand what he is thinking? Not easy, but possible. So, to begin, we encounter what we might think of as a strange way of referring to God — "In the beginning was the Word, and the word was with God and the word was God (John 1:1)" — God is called the word (or in Greek, the λόγος — *Logos*). That *is* strange to us, but it was not at all strange to either Jews or Greeks in the first century.

For Jewish readers, the term word was regularly used as a way of denoting God without actually using the divine name. It went all the way back to the stories of the beginning of the universe as the scriptures said that everything created was brought into being simply by God's say-so... the word. Every Jew was used to talking about the Memra — the word of God. It did not mean holy scripture; it meant God.

But for Greek readers, it was an even more highly thought out concept. It had been worked out hundreds of years before by the philosopher Heraclitus. His basic idea was that everything was in a state of flux: everything was changing from day to day and from moment to moment. His famous illustration was that it was impossible to step twice into the same river. You step into a river; you step out; you step in again... but you do not step into the same river because the water has flowed on — thus, it is a different river each time you step in.

To Heraclitus everything was like that; everything was in a constant state of flux. But, if that is so, why is life not complete chaos? How can there be any sense to a world where there is constant change? Heraclitus' answer was that all this change and flux was not haphazard — it was controlled and ordered and followed a continuous pattern all the time... and what controlled it all was the logos, the word, or another way of translating it, the logic (which, of course, has its root in logos) or the reason of God. To Heraclitus, the logos was the principle of order under which the universe continued to exist.

The philosopher brought the matter even nearer to home. What was it that told us as individuals the difference between right and wrong? What gave us the ability to think and sort things out? What enabled us to recognize truth? Once again, Heraclitus gave the same answer: the *logos*... the word, dwelling within.

The Jews knew about the logos; the Greeks knew about the logos; no one had any problem with the concept of a God who controlled all things. But now Jesus comes along — "the Word became flesh and lived among us." Most first-century Christians affirmed that, in a unique way, Jesus is the word... the logos... come to earth.

All well? Hardly. The Greeks had a terrible time with it. The one thing that no Greek would have ever dreamed was that God could take a body. To the Greek, the body was evil... a prison-house for the soul, a tomb in which the spirit was confined. Matter itself was evil. Thus, many Greeks did not believe that God directly controlled the affairs of this world: God exercised control through intermediaries, "lesser gods," or emanations because God could not be "soiled" by becoming directly involved in physical affairs. The *logos* could not become *flesh*!

Some of the early Christians had trouble with the concept too, so there arose within the church a group known as the Docetists. They got their name from the Greek word *dok eó* which means to seem. They held that Jesus only seemed to be really human — that his human body was not a real body; that he could not feel hunger or weariness, sorrow or pain; that he was in fact a disembodied spirit in the apparent form of a man. Jesus was a phantom. That kind of thinking resulted in stories like, "When Jesus walked, he left no footprints," or "When Jesus was crucified, he was not really up there on that cross at all; in fact, while the crucifixion was going on, Jesus was seen talking to some of his disciples on the Mount of Olives." The stories were not true, of course, but they arose because the Docetists had as much a problem as the other Greeks with the logos becoming flesh.

I would love to tell you that, even though some folks had questions, everything was worked out on a Sunday morning in the fellowship hall over coffee and donuts as people satisfied themselves that the details could be dealt with later. Ha! There were literally battles in the streets over this issue and they continued for years and years. The issue was not settled in the church until the Council of Nicea in the middle of the fifth century when a creed was agreed to that affirmed that Jesus was both 100% God and 100% human without explaining how such was possible.[17] In essence, the creed says that whatever God is, Jesus is; and whatever humanity is, Jesus is that too, in one whole person. We do not pretend to understand all that, because Christ is unique — we have no one with whom to compare him.

By the way, just as history is written by the winners, so is theology. Those who said Jesus was *both* human and divine had the most votes in the council, and that has been the position of the church ever since. Winner, winner, chicken dinner.

As we are sadly aware, theological controversies arise constantly. I remember Mark Twain's reflection on the problem. He described a fictitious experiment. He said, "In an hour, I taught a dog and a cat to be friends. I put them in a cage. In another hour I taught them to be friends with a rabbit. In the course of two days, I was able to add a fox, a goose, a squirrel,

17. For a succinct and very readable summary of the story, read about the Nicene Creed online. In my library I have Jack Rogers, *Presbyterian Creeds, A Guide to the Book of Confessions*, (Philadelphia: Westminster Press, 1985) which provides a most readable account of the controversies and ultimate settlement.

and some doves. Finally, I added a monkey. They lived together in peace... even affectionately. Next, in another cage, I put an Irish Catholic from Tipperary, and as soon as he seemed tame, I added a Scotch Presbyterian from Aberdeen. Next a Turk from Constantinople, a Greek Christian from Crete, an Armenian, a Methodist from the wilds of Arkansas, a Buddhist from China, a Brahmin from India, and finally, a Salvation Army Colonel. Then I stayed away for two whole days. When I came back the cage of animals was all right, but the other was a chaos of gory odds and ends of fezzes and turbans and plaids and bone and flesh... not a specimen left alive. They had disagreed on a theological detail and taken the matter to a higher court."[18]

"And the word became flesh and lived among us." What *should* we say about Jesus?[19] The story opens with the birth of a baby in an out-of-the-way town called Bethlehem with his first cradle a manger for the feeding of livestock. He grew up in the unsanitary mountain village of Nazareth with a reputation only for the fact that nothing "good" had ever come from that town. As far as we can tell, it was a normal home; Jesus would have shared normal duties with his brothers and sisters. He knew how to fill lamps and to trim wicks. He knew what housecleaning involved. He knew how to build a fire and could prepare a fish fry. He learned the trade of a carpenter. In other words, a real person, not some figure out of ancient mythology. Flesh and bone, muscle and blood. Real — but also special!

We believe in "God, the Father..." and that, in a special way, we are all God's children. But the church also insists that Jesus is unique. Listen to the writer of the epistle to the Hebrews: *"Long ago God spoke to our ancestors in many and various ways by the prophets, but in these last days he has spoken to us by a Son, whom he appointed heir of all things, through whom he also created the worlds. He is the reflection of God's glory and the exact imprint of God's very being, and he sustains all things by his powerful word." (Hebrews 1:1-3)*

That is no description of you or me. If Jesus is God's only son, does that put the rest of us down? No. Exactly the opposite, in fact. The very idea that Jesus would take on flesh and blood and become one of us is incredible and elevates us beyond measure.

---

18. *Mark Twain Tonight*, directed by David Susskind, aired March 6, 1967, on CBS.
19. For a more complete consideration of this question, I refer you to my book *As We Believe, So We Behave: Living the Apostles' Creed* (Lima, Ohio: CSS Publishing, 2008) and the chapter "Jesus Christ, our Lord," p 41.

Yes, we believe he was a real person, both human and divine, God's only son. We also believe he was Jesus Christ. At about thirty years of age, Jesus laid aside the tools of his trade and began to teach and preach and heal. From the beginning people reacted to him. Little children ran to him at the sound of his voice, the aged found comfort in his presence, the sick found healing by merely touching the hem of his garment.

He had his hours of popularity when the multitudes gathered 'round. He had his moments of quiet reflection, either alone or with those closest to him. It was on just such an occasion that we encounter the dialogue between Jesus and the twelve, "Who do you say that I am?" Simon answers, "You are the Messiah (from the Hebrew), [or] the Christ (the Greek equivalent of Messiah), the Son of the living God" (Matthew 16:16).

Christ is not Jesus' surname. It is a title. It indicates "the anointed one" — someone set apart for God's service. This was God's representative. In the Old Testament the title was regularly applied to the king. By the time of Jesus, the Jewish people were looking for a Messiah, a Christ, to come who would lead them in victory against their oppressors, a conquering hero who would overthrow the hated Romans. As soon became evident, this was not God's intention in Jesus. For those who had their hopes pinned on a military Messiah, this was a devastating blow. Indeed, some have speculated that this was Judas' problem – once he found out that his dream of conquest was over, he bolted ranks. And the rest of the story we know too well.

Jesus was betrayed by those he trusted, abandoned by those he loved. A purple robe was thrown contemptuously across his shoulders, a crown of thorns jammed down upon his brow. He carried his own cross, as far as he was able, to an outlaw's execution. The life which had begun in humble obscurity ended in public shame. He who, at birth, had been laid in a borrowed manger was now laid away in a borrowed tomb.

But we know the story does not end there. And that is why we can continue to affirm, "I believe in Jesus Christ... our Lord!"

Lord — what does the name mean? To the ancients it meant master or owner and was always a title of consummate respect. In the modern world, to call Jesus "Lord" is to say he is the chief, the boss, the main man, the head honcho. The buck stops with him; his decisions are final.

Jesus Christ is Lord! These four words were the first creed that the Christian church ever had. In fact, it is those four words that comprise the basic confession of the church, regardless of denomination. To be a Christian then and to be a Christian now is to make that affirmation.

If someone can say, "For me, Jesus Christ is Lord," that person is a Christian.

No question, we are grateful for it. We know from John Calvin that if Jesus were not God, he could not save us; but if Jesus were not man, he could not reach us. Still, it is a mystery.

Then why fool with it if it is all that complicated? Why not just let the professional theologians wrestle with it along with questions like "How many angels can dance on the head of a pin?" Well, for several reasons: one is that we learn something about God here; another is that we learn something about ourselves; and finally we learn something about the mission of the church.

Concerning God, we learn that the ancient Greeks (and indeed many who have followed their thinking), with their concept of a God who could not possibly be involved in human affairs, were wrong. God was and is involved to the extent of dealing so intimately with creation as to actually become a part of it. God is not aloof; God did not just wind the world up like a clock and then let it go spinning on its way. And if God were like that 2,000 years ago, we can affirm that God is no less interested and involved in our day. Despite all our worries about the evils of this world — despite our concerns about poverty, hunger, nuclear proliferation, and the like — the mystery of the word becoming flesh comes through to us and says we have not been abandoned, nor will we ever be.

Concerning ourselves, we learn that, in the eyes of almighty God, it is all right to be human. The message is that the body is not simply the prison-house of the soul... that, in spite of the fact of our sinful natures, true humanity, human life lived as God originally intended, is something very special, special enough for God to become human one magnificent night in Bethlehem.

Concerning our mission as a church, we learn that God came into the world in human flesh for a reason. Jesus said at the beginning of his earthly ministry as he quoted Isaiah the prophet, "The Spirit of the Lord is upon me, because he has anointed me to bring good news to the poor. He has sent me to proclaim freedom for the prisoners and recovery of sight for the blind, to release the oppressed, to proclaim the year of the Lord's favor" (Luke 4:18-19). Then in John's gospel, He makes it clear that *his* task is no less *our* task: "Even as the Father has sent me, I am sending you" (John 20:21). Because of what we know about the incarnation, the "enfleshment" of God, we know something about our mission in the world.

Yes, Christmas is a time of joy and celebration... and especially for children. All of us can join them in that. But for those of us who are no longer children, the story of Christmas means so much more. In a special way, a mysterious way, the human and divine are intertwined, and with reverence we can affirm, "And the Word became flesh..."

O Word of God, Incarnate,
O Wisdom from on high,
O Truth unchanged, unchanging,
O light of our dark sky;
We praise Thee for the radiance,
That from the hallowed page,
A lantern to our footsteps,
Shines on from age to age.[20]

Amen!

---

20. William Walsham Howe, 1867, in the public domain.

Baptism Of The Lord

Mark 1:4-11

I Am Somebody!

I suspect that, having made it to mid-January, you would say that you have successfully survived the holidays. True? The celebration of our Savior's birth — Christmas; then the New Year; finally the Feast of the Three Kings on January 6th — Epiphany (which for many has become the Feast of Taking Down the Decorations!). Today I want to suggest that there is one more holiday we should be observing — this day, the one the liturgical calendar designates to remember the Baptism of the Lord.

If the witness of scripture is to be taken seriously, this day must be even more important than those others. After all, only Matthew and Luke record anything about Jesus' birth, but all four gospels report his baptism, plus Acts and Romans. In fact, in centuries past the church did celebrate this day even more than the days remembering the holy birth, but we have drifted away from that practice — sad. Because, in the process, we have relegated to minor importance an event that, when properly understood, can give us a sense of enthusiasm, encouragement, and absolute joy.

Think about the scene for a moment. We are down by the riverside of the Jordan. There is a throng of people from all walks of life who have made this mini-pilgrimage into the countryside. They have come to see an itinerant preacher who is more than passing strange — a coarse camel's hair tunic with a leather belt around his waist, the uniform of a prophet since the days of Elijah (2 Kings 1:8). It was longing and anticipation that brought this mass of people out — there was a sense that something was missing in their walk with God, so they were ready to listen to a new voice.

And this is a powerful voice: "You pack of snakes! Who warned you to run from the anger of God that is coming on you? Clean up your act! And do not presume to rely on that fact that you are Israelites — God's chosen people – to save you. Get right and do right." The crowds asked what to do. He responded, "Whoever has two coats must share with anyone who has none; and whoever has food must do likewise." Tax collectors were told, "Collect no more than the amount prescribed for you." Soldiers were instructed, "Do not extort money from anyone by threats or false accusation, and be satisfied with your wages."[21] It was a message that affirmed what they already knew: if they would be right with God, they had to be right with not only God, but God's children as well. Then as a sign of their commitment to repentance and a new way of living, they made their way down into the river, allowed John to "bury" their old ways under the water in baptism, then raise them again to a better life. It is a neat ceremony with wonderful symbolism. And in the hands of a dynamic personality... so forceful and impressive that some were led to think that John was the promised Messiah finally come. He debunked that notion out of hand: "After me will come one more powerful than I, the thongs of whose sandals I am not worthy to stoop down and untie. I baptize you with water, but he will baptize you with the Holy Spirit."

Then one day it happened... Jesus. The request for baptism. John's initial reluctance, then acquiescence. Finally, the dramatic climax. As our lesson has it, "As Jesus was coming up out of the water, he saw heaven being torn apart and the Spirit descending on him like a dove. And a voice came from heaven: "You are my Son, the beloved; with you I am well pleased." What an image! It is as if God the Father is confined to heaven at this fantastic moment and in euphoric frustration rips and tears the very fabric of the universe to lay claim upon the son. It is a cosmic yes, arms raised high and feet dancing. It is love spilling out, the cup overflowing. Not celebrating the conclusion of a work-well-done, but before anything was done, and now about to embark on his ministry.

This changed everything! Jesus' baptism ushered in a new baptism. Christian baptism became not just a washing away of sin, as John's baptism was, but the baptism that brings the power of the Holy Spirit and a special relationship with God.[22] Why? For no reason other than God chooses to do it. That is worth a holiday in my book.

Perhaps we should be used to this by now, but once more, all our high and holy religious expectations are trashed. It started with the ruler of the entire universe entering this world how? As an all-powerful potentate? No. An utterly helpless infant. The king of creation being born where? A palace? No. Among the animals. As life went on his best

21. The details of John's instruction come from the account in Luke's gospel, Luke 3:7-14.
22. Brian Stoffregen, *Gospel Notes for Next Sunday*, volume no. 2764, (January 5, 1997), Ecunet.

friends were whom? The privileged and powerful? No. The down and dirty, the outcasts, those on life's fringes. And, of course, at the end of it all here, instead of doing the really smart thing and not dying, he dies. Then three days later, *surprise*! Why should we be startled when we learn that God loves us for no more reason than good parents do: *just because*.

This is only half of the message from Jesus' baptism and our own — we are loved. Most folks understand that, and that is why they get all warm and fuzzy when it comes to presenting their little ones for the sacrament. But there is another half, and it is this: we have work to do. Remember, this happened at the start of Jesus' work. This was his commissioning service. Now, over twenty centuries later, when someone is baptized in the church (infants or adults), it is no different. There is surely the affirmation of God's incredible and unconditional love and... and this is a big and... a commissioning to service in the name of Jesus Christ. That is why we take so seriously the promises that new disciples make or their parents make on their behalf — to live the Christian faith, to teach that faith to the children. We even go for extra help: we ask the congregation, "Do you, as members of the church of Jesus Christ, promise to guide and nurture, by word and deed, with love and prayer, encouraging these new disciples to know and follow Christ and to be faithful members of his church?"[23] New disciples have work to do, and they will need all the help they can get.

Both of the elements are important: the affirmation of affection and the proclamation of purpose. Lacking one or the other, we are incomplete.

Among the millions of Jews imprisoned by the Nazis in the death camps of the thirties and forties was Victor Frankl. In spite of the horrors and the odds, he survived. Around him, next to him, each day of his ordeal, dozens, hundreds, thousands of fellow Jews and others died, many of them, of course, in the ovens — but many others were killed by giving up hope, losing heart, overwhelmed by horror and fear and hopelessness. Frankl survived, he said, because two forces sustained him: one was the certainty of his wife's love. The other was an inner drive to rewrite the manuscript of a book he had completed after years of labor — but the Nazis had destroyed. Frankl's imprisonment was lightened by daily imaginary conversations with his wife and by

---

23. This is part of the liturgy in the author's tradition, the Presbyterian Church (USA). *Book of Common Worship*, (Louisville, KY, Westminster/ John Knox Press, 1995) p. 406. Different traditions may handle the process in their own ways.

scrawling notes for his book on all the bits and scraps of paper he could find. Now Frankl has written eloquently of these two insights to cope with life: first, the discovery and certainty of being loved, and, second, having a clear and controlling purpose in life.[24] Both are the messages we receive in Christian baptism.

One of my cyber-friends wrote,[25] "I think of the story that appeared a few years ago in the midst of the upheaval in the former Soviet Union about the fact that Gorbachev's grandmother had had him baptized as an infant, and what that meant as far as his willingness to see and do things differently. I think of the conversion and baptism of the former slave trader, John Newton, and his ministry of healing and grace which continues through his hymns. I think of how important Luther's remembrance that 'I am baptized' was to him in moments of trial and despair... I will be honest. I tremble and grow weak when I do baptisms... and I weep. Not because of some cute-little-baby-warm-fuzzy-isn't-this-a-nice-family picture kind of feeling, but because I think it is the most radical and dangerous thing I do. And maybe because it is so radical, so dangerous, so threatening, that people either flee the church as they get older, or they weep when we have the opportunity to reaffirm our baptismal vows."

One of our most eloquent writers has asked, "Does anyone have the foggiest idea what sort of power we so blithely invoke? Or, as I suspect, does no one believe a word of it? The churches are children playing on the floor with their chemistry sets, mixing up a batch of TNT to kill a Sunday morning. It is madness to wear ladies' straw hats and velvet gloves to church; we should all be wearing crash helmets..."[26]

The baptism of the Lord was a big deal, and much bigger than we have given it credit for in its implications for you and me. Perhaps if we celebrated this day as a holiday... a holy day... we might reclaim the importance of the sacrament. After all, what we do in those sacred moments at the font has the potential for unleashing incredible power. The message is that you are loved and you have a purpose; that combination makes you very special.

You are all familiar with the Rev. Jesse Jackson. No matter what folks think of Jesse's politics, most everyone will agree that he is an incredible speaker. Jesse speaks in many different settings, and one of those he enjoys the most is school auditoriums — he loves addressing

24. Nate Castens, *Gospel Notes for Next Sunday*, no. 2815, (January 10, 1997). Ecunet.
25. Thom M. Shuman, *Sermonshop*, no. 92 (January 9, 1997), PresbyNet.
26. Annie Dillard, *Teaching A Stone To Talk*, (New York: Harper Perennial, 1982) p. 58.

students, particularly those who come from disadvantaged backgrounds, to give them a sense of their own worth, a new self-esteem, and a vision of a better future. Some years ago, he began concluding his speeches by having the youngsters respond to his urgings with a litany of self-affirmation. He would say something or ask some question and the kids would respond, "I am somebody!" Over and over again, the youngsters would be asked about themselves and the response would be, "I am somebody." By the time Jesse would be done, those students would be positively bellowing, "I am somebody," and they would leave with a sense of worth that, for many, would be brand new.

The message of your baptism and my baptism is that, in God's grand scheme of things, *I am somebody... you are somebody.*

The world asks, "Who are you?" and because of your baptism you can proudly proclaim, I am somebody.

The world says we have no interest in you, but you can say, "World, you had better," because you can audaciously affirm, "I am somebody!"

Your detractors can say they can ignore you, but because of your baptism, you can say, "You dare not, because I am somebody!"

Society says we have no need of you, but you can say, "Oh, yes, you do, because I am somebody!"

On this day, many Christians in congregations around the world will reaffirm their baptisms. Then, you can tell me whether or not this day that recalls of the baptism of the Lord deserves a holiday. I think absolutely! Because at its heart it teaches me that my own baptism says, in spite of all my fears and failures, any worry and wonder, once and for all, in the eyes of the God of all the universe, I can say that I am somebody!

Amen!

Epiphany 2
John 1:43-51

Come And See

I have always liked this story — and not for the WHOLE story, just that one memorable line: "Can anything good come out of Nazareth? (John 1:46)" That is just the kind of snide comment that makes me smirk. And, to be quite honest, it is one of the things that I like about our scripture — it is honest. Over and over and over again, the pages of our holy writ are littered with snide comments, unfaithful friends, ugly confrontations and some of the most unsavory "saints" that anyone could ever imagine. But God uses them. And that gives me hope because if God can use all of that hot mess, God can use even a fool like me. Hallelujah!

To Philip's credit, he does not take offense at his friend's remark. He ignores it and invites him "Come and see." So Nathanael did, and the rest, as they say, is history. Good for him — and good for Philip too. He had found something good and he wanted to share. That's what friends are for. Right?

Is that how you came to faith? A faithful Mom or Dad? A caring Sunday school teacher or youth leader? A friend? That *is* the way most of us were introduced to Jesus.

I need all the friends I can get! You do too. Everyone does. An old Italian proverb asks, "Have you fifty friends? It is not enough. Have you one enemy? It is too many." Socrates once said, "All people have their different objects of ambition — horses, dogs, money, honor, as the case may be, but for my part I would rather have a good friend than all these put together."[27]

Unfortunately, we are such a mobile society that we rarely make close friends, and those we do make in many cases are now far away from us. We have acquaintances galore — golf buddies, bridge partners, folks we slap on the back at Rotary or Kiwanis. Those are all well and good. But real friends? Ones we can laugh with, cry with, share the deepest of feelings? No. In fact, a national business magazine has

27. Socrates, Quoted in Leonard Griffith, *The Eternal Legacy from an Upper Room*, (New York: Harper & Row, 1963), p. 137

suggested, "Friendship Can Ruin Your Business."[28] The author of the article argued that executives should keep a sharp watch over social patterns in the office — excessive friendliness would impair efficiency. He went on to say that "precautionary watchfulness will prevent an up-and-coming manager from carrying around his neck a millstone of personal commitments, loyalties and friendships." Friendship a burden? Please.

According to a survey by the Yankelovich organization sometime back, 70% of Americans recognize that, while they have many acquaintances, they have few close friends, and they say that is a serious void in their lives. How about you? Would you like to have more and better friends, friends like Philip who would invite you to come and see? Consider the issue with me for a few minutes.

First, if you want real friends, you have to care about people. Jesus said, "This is my commandment, that you love one another as I have loved you." The love he meant was not a warm, fuzzy feeling, but a consistent interest in the other person's welfare along with a desire to do whatever is necessary to see that his or her wellbeing is maintained. That is the biblical understanding of love. Not romance, but an unfailing interest and care. It is basic to any worthwhile relationship.

In my files, I have an old Miss Manners' column from the newspaper. She was responding to a letter from a grandmother who was concerned that people were intimidated by her or thought she was conceited or a know-it-all. Grandma then proceeded to describe how she had plenty of money, grew award-winning roses, was currently working on a novel and two master's degrees, is "interested" in everything, noted that she was proud of her accomplishments and wanted to let everyone know about them. Miss Manners responded, "Dear, dear. I can see your problem," and then went on to let this lady know that if she really were interested in everything, she might think of being interested in other people and their accomplishments — she wrote, "they will be twice as impressed if they find out accidentally what you have done."[29] Good advice. As that wonderful old rhyme has it,

28. Quoted by C. Thomas Hilton, "Known By Our Friends," *The Clergy Journal*, April, 1992, p. 14.
29. Judith Martin, "Energetic Grandma Needs to Change Focus," *Fort Myers News-Press*, March 15, 1990.

I went out to find a friend,
But could not find one there;
I went out to be a friend,
And friends were everywhere.

Part of that care, that love, for other people is a willingness to put yourself out, to sacrifice. Christ made it clear when he said, "No one has greater love than this, to lay down one's life for one's friends."

Something within us has always responded to the old Greek legend of Damon and Pythias: Damon condemned to death and Pythias offering to stand as a guarantee for him while his friend returned home to put his affairs in order; Damon's ship delayed and Pythias praying for unfavorable winds that he might be allowed to die in his friend's place; Damon arriving at the last minute and the two friends arguing as to which should be privileged to die for the other. That is true friendship — a willingness to spend oneself for the other ungrudgingly and without counting the cost.[30]

To be sure, we are rarely called on to die for our friends (thank goodness), but the message is clear: real friendship involves a willingness to go the extra mile when necessary (and even when not necessary). Being a real friend is work. It takes time. Sometimes it is painful. As has been said, "Some people make enemies instead of friends because it is less trouble" (E. C. McKenzie). Too bad. They do not know what they are missing.

Another key to having friends is a willingness to communicate. That is why Jesus made the distinction between servants and friends. To be sure, being a servant of the Lord is a high honor — the Bible calls some of the greatest people in history by that title: Abraham, Moses, Joshua, Paul. But perhaps Jesus was thinking of the practice in oriental courts where a select group of intimates were known as "friends of the king" or "friends of the emperor." In ancient days, these friends had special access to the sovereign at all times, even the right come into the royal apartments at the beginning of the day. The king talked with them before he talked with his generals, his legislators, his statesmen. He confided to them the deepest purposes of his heart and heard their advice. Others were servants; these were friends.[31] There was special communication between them.

---

30. Leonard Griffith, *The Eternal Legacy,*. 141-142.
31. Griffith, *The Eternal Legacy*, 138.

Real communication is not easy though. It involves a willingness to open up even if the revelations about ourselves might not be so pleasant. My roommate and traveling companion while I was working on my doctorate some years ago, Clark Wiser, once told me that he had gone into his young son's room for bedtime prayers. But instead of welcoming his dad as he normally did, Andrew turned his head to the wall and began praying in an inaudible mumble. Clark asked, "Andrew, what's the matter?"

"Nothing."

"Well, something is the matter. Why don't you want me to hear your prayers? You can tell me."

"No, I can't. Tonight I can only tell them to the Lord — he won't get mad with me."

A highly respected marriage and family therapist mentioned an experience one couple had in their counseling sessions. The husband broke down and said, "You know what it is? All these years I've been scared to death that someday she'll break through my shell and realize what an idiot I really am." Friends allow each other to be the idiots we really are.[32] Someone has defined a friend as a person who knows us and likes us anyway.

Another key to developing friendships is a willingness to cooperate. That is why Jesus said, "You are my friends if you do what I command you (love each other)." He went on to say that, as a friend, he will respond to our requests: "I chose you and I appointed you to go and bear fruit, fruit that will last, so that the Father will give you whatever you ask him in in my name." (John 15:14, 16) The message here is that friends play on the same team, use the same strategies, aim for the same goal. They are not at cross-purposes with each other. Some have read these words, "Whatever you ask in my name, the Father will give it," and figured that Christians are being offered a blank check. But then they find that their prayers are not always answered the way they had anticipated. That cooperation of purpose is the reason.

I will never forget being with my daughter Erin hearing her prayers one night many years ago. Her kindergarten class had been learning about the destruction of the rainforest (she is old enough to have her own kindergartners now). Her prayer that night was "Dear God, those people who are cutting down all the trees in the rainforest? Please kill them." From a five-year-old that might be expected, but there are some adult prayers that are equally off the wall simply because they are at

32. Tom Hilton, "Known by Our Friends," p. 16.

cross purposes with what the Lord, in divine wisdom, knows to be best.

Real friendship starts with caring; it is willing to sacrifice; it communicates; it cooperates. It is intriguing that Jesus starts this little instruction with the command to love each other, then, within a few sentences, He ends with "I am giving you these commands so that you may love one another." For all that people might do to analyze friendship, the Lord's word is that it starts and ends with simple caring.

One of the fundamental and irrefutable facts of human nature is this: none of us is an island. We desperately need the strength and security which comes from having friends who care about us and who are willing to let us care about them. As the writer of Ecclesiastes has it, "Two are better than one... if they fall, one will lift up the other; but woe to one who is alone and does not have another to help" (Ecclesiastes 4:9-10).

The good news of the gospel is that every one of us has at least one abiding friend, Jesus Christ. "You are my friends if you do what I command you... not servants... friends." Earthly companions come and go, but this one remains for all eternity. You see, at heart, a Christian is nothing more than someone who has accepted the friendship of Jesus.

It has been truly said that Jesus could go into any factory or farm, into any office or classroom, and his presence would not make people uncomfortable. In fact, his next visit would be eagerly looked for. Why? Because in his presence men and women felt their inner, better selves revived within them. Jesus lifted their hearts. He saw all their dormant possibilities, and he made the people see their true potential. What is more, he made them desire, with a deep and passionate longing, that those possibilities should become real and his dreams for them come true; he made folks believe they could come true, and that life could be full and warm and beautiful.

The friendship of Jesus. How can we get it? There are no conditions to it other than the faith that such a wonderful thing is possible. Where do we find it? Some would try to say, "Anywhere. Just look around." But the reality is that RIGHT HERE is where we find it — in the fellowship of Christians. That is why the Bible calls the church "the Body of Christ." For all the church's faults, this is still the place for people to come to find the friendship of Jesus.

Once I heard of a Sunday school teacher who had a little lad in her class who had no right hand. She was exceedingly sensitive about any activities that she would schedule for the youngsters so as not to make this one uncomfortable. After a few months of having him in the class, she began to notice his handicap less and less and take him simply as part of the group. One day in an effort to illustrate what the church was all about, she tried to demonstrate and have the youngsters mimic that little gesture that we all learned when we were growing up. She put her hands together — this is the church, this is the steeple, open the doors and here are all... Then she realized. She was aghast at her faux pas until she saw the little girl who was sitting next to the boy extend her right hand over toward his left hand and say, "Here, we can do it together."

That sounds like something Jesus would do. That is the kind of friendship that the Lord's church is about. That is the friendship that, empowered by the love of Christ, we offer to each other. That is the friendship that is offered to all the world. That is the friendship that is offered to you and me.

Philip was a wonderful friend to Nathanael. "We have found him about whom Moses in the law and also the prophets wrote, Jesus son of Joseph from Nazareth."

Nathanael said to him, "Can anything good come out of Nazareth?"

Philip said to him, "Come and see." And that invitation, that friendship, changed his life.

Amen.

Epiphany 3

Mark 1:14-20

Let's Go Fishing!

An old-timer sat on the river bank, obviously awaiting a nibble, though the fishing season had not officially opened. A uniformed officer stood behind him quietly for several minutes. "You the game warden?" the old-timer inquired.

"Yup."

Unruffled, the old man began to move the fishing pole from side to side. Finally, he lifted the line out of the water. Pointing to a minnow wriggling on the end of the line, he said, "Just teaching him how to swim."[33]

Mark Twain once spent a pleasant three weeks in the Maine woods but as he was now on his way home, making himself comfortable in the train on the way back to New York, a sour-faced New Englander sat down next to him, and the two struck up a conversation. "Been to the woods, have ye?" asked the stranger.

"I have indeed," replied Twain. "And let me tell you something. It may be closed season for fishing up here in Maine, but I have a couple of hundred pounds of the finest rock bass you ever saw iced down in the baggage car. By the way, who are you, sir?"

"I'm the state game warden. Who are you?" was the reply.

Said Twain, "Pleased to meet you. Who am I? Only the biggest liar in these United States."[34]

Two ardent fishermen met on their vacation and began swapping stories about the different places they had fished, the kind of tackle used, the best bait, and finally about some of the fish they had caught. One of them told of a vicious battle he once had with a 300-pound salmon. The other man listened attentively. He frankly admitted he had never caught anything quite that big. However, he told about the time his hook snagged a lantern from the depths of a lake. The lantern carried a tag proving it was lost back in 1912. But the strangest thing of all was the fact that it was a waterproof lantern and the light was still lit.

33 Jacob M. Braude, *Braude's Treasury of Humor*, (Englewood Cliffs, NJ: Prentice-Hall, 1964), 78.
34. James C. Humes, *Podium Humor*, (New York: Harper & Row, 1975), 189-190.

For a long time the first man said nothing. Then he took one long deep breath. "I'll tell you what I'll do," he said slowly. "I'll take 200 pounds off my fish, if you'll put out the light in your lantern."[35]

Fishing stories — you gotta love 'em. What brings them to mind this morning is this gospel lesson with Jesus' call to four fishermen who he says he will make into "fishers of men." A few notes. First, the players: Simon, Andrew, James, and John — names with which the world has become familiar over two millennia of Christian history — but, in their own day, just average folks. It was Abraham Lincoln who said, "God must love the common people — He made so many of them."[36] And the selection of these first disciples is just one more affirmation that God uses common people — just like you and me — to get the work of the kingdom done. A bit scary for us, perhaps, because we are talking big responsibility here. But more on that in a minute.

Where were these folks when Jesus called them? Church? Synagogue? Some spiritual retreat? No. They were at work — catching fish, mending nets — going about their normal routine. Jesus is not limited to church; he can and often does meet us in the midst of our everyday lives.

What did Jesus call them to do? "Follow me." Not worship me... *follow* me. Tag along. "Hang" with me. No doubt these men had encountered this fascinating preacher before. It would not be surprising to learn that they had stood in the crowds that had been listening to Jesus and listened right along, we would not be surprised to hear that they had stayed to talk long after the crowd began to drift away. They had been impressed. Perhaps there is a lesson there in how folks become disciples. Just being around Jesus. Picking up on the things that Jesus thinks are important. Seeing what Jesus cares about... and what he gets upset about. Learning what his priorities are. The more time we spend with Jesus — prayer, Bible study, the fellowship of the body of Christ —the better disciples we become.

One more point to note: Jesus had a task for them. I will make you fishers of men! You have some skills already; now put them to work in the service of the kingdom! And this is the primary task of Christian disciples — cast the nets, bait the hooks, reach outside of the boat. I wish I could say that the church through the centuries has taken that task seriously, but we know better. Perhaps we would improve if we analyzed the problem and then found some ways to do a better job and

35. Jacob Braude, *Braude's Treasury*, 78..
36. Abraham Lincoln, quoted by William Barclay, *The Gospel of Mark, Daily Study Bible Series*, (Philadelphia: Westminster, 1956), 19.

handle this big responsibility we mentioned a moment ago.

From the beginning, Christianity was a lay movement, common people filled with the great conviction that Jesus Christ was Lord, God in human flesh. Those lay people made that conviction known to everyone with whom they came in contact and made such an impact that, within just a few years, people could say of them, "These people who have been turning the world upside down have come here also" (Acts 17:6). If the church is ever to accomplish the mission Jesus outlined at the beginning, the task of being "fishers of men," it will be through the efforts of consecrated people who, no matter what their occupation, respond to the Lord's call to evangelize the world. It's time for church people to stop wringing their hands and start ringing doorbells.

Admittedly, some will never do it. A minister wearing his clerical collar was having lunch in a restaurant down the street from his church. The man at the table next to him asked, "I see you are a minister; where is your church?"

The minister replied, "I serve the church right up the street."

The man responded, "Hey, that's *my* church too. Small world."

The minister said, "I have been pastor there for two years now; I am sorry to say I don't recall having seen you there."

The man responded, "Reverend, I said I was a member, not a fanatic." Thank God that those Jesus called from their fishing boats did not feel that way.

Now, I freely admit that I know a lot more about many things than fishing, but even one who has spent little time with a rod and reel can see a few basics. For example, you cannot catch any fish if there are none to be caught. It makes sense — and that is the excuse many folks use to not "fish for people" — they say they do not know anyone who is not already "caught," already a part of Christ's church. Perhaps. At least at some time in the past, perhaps. But the sad truth is that, even here in the most overtly religious nation in the technologically advanced world, half the people you and I know are effectively unchurched. That means that they have not attended worship, other than a Christmas or an Easter, a wedding or funeral, at any time in the past six months. If you are worried about there being no fish out there, don't. There are gracious plenty.

Another basic: it helps to know when the fish are biting. Some TV weathercasters even give the best times of the day for anglers to be out on the water. How about the "fish" that Jesus sends us after? One of the best opportunities is at a moment of transition. Perhaps a birth or a death, new home, new job, or these days, *no* job. One cyberfriend of mine wrote,

> *The dedicated fishermen in my parish... are ever watchful and sensitive to change – they watch the currents in the water, sniff the air for moisture, aware of changes in weather as lows and highs invade the atmosphere, watch the terrain under the boat looking for habitat that contain the fish. And they change – when the circumstances change going deeper in the water, switching lures when light intensity in the water changes or when they are in clear water vs. darker water.*[37]

Good lesson for those who "fish for people" as well. Be sensitive to the changes in people's lives that might make them hungry for a word of good news.

Speaking of hunger, that brings to mind another basic: bait. You have to have something to attract the fish. It might be a flashy lure or some mouthwateringly scrumptious worm (gag), but to expect the fish to just jump in the boat for no reason will not work. If you want to be successful as you "fish for people" you will offer something to attract new disciples of God, same as one would for fish. For example, an invitation to "Come to church with me sometime" will rarely work. It is too easy to say "Sure" to that and never give it another thought. Instead, invite your friend to something particular: a special event or a distinctive worship service (Ash Wednesday, Palm Sunday, Maundy Thursday, Mother's Day), some outstanding program. Be creative, but be specific. That way someone must actually make a decision, rather than put you off with a meaningless "Sure."

By the way, there is an ancillary bit of advice for those of you reluctant people-fishers who are afraid you might be using the wrong bait; in other words, saying the wrong thing. Worry not! God can and does use the strangest witnesses to accomplish the kingdom's purpose.

I love this story.[38] This man was not well educated and his manner was somewhat rough and crude, but he became a Christian and took his commitment seriously. He kept pestering his pastor to put him to

37. G. Duane Baun, *Gospel Notes for Next Sunday*, no. 2946, (January 24, 1997), Ecunet.
38. David E. Leininger, *Lectionary Tales for the Pulpit*, Series VI, Cycle A, (Lima, OH: CSS Publishing, 2007), 35.

work. Finally, the minister handed him a list of ten names with this explanation: "These are all members of the church, but they seldom attend. Some of them are prominent people in the community. Contact them about being more faithful. Here is some church stationary to write letters. Get them back in church."

The man accepted the challenge with rugged determination and enthusiasm. About three weeks later a letter from a prominent physician whose name had been on the list arrived at the church office. Inside was a large check and a brief note: "Dear Pastor, Enclosed is my check for $1,000 to help make up for my missing church so much, but be assured that I will be present this Lord's Day and each Lord's Day following. I will not by choice miss services again. Sincerely... P.S. Would you please tell your secretary that there is only one 'T' in dirty and no 'C' in Skunk."

One final bit of fishing advice (and I say final only because of time considerations – whole books of advice for anglers are out there). Be patient. Fishing requires perseverance. If you give up after a few minutes, a few casts, without any bites or nibbles, you will never catch any fish. 'Tis the same in fishing for people: you have to keep on casting, keep on extending the invitation, sometimes adjusting the bait. Give your efforts time to make an impact, then let the Holy Spirit do the rest.

"Follow me," says Jesus, "and I will make you fish for people." Are you ready to cast out? The word is that there are fish, lots of them... lots more than we might suspect. What are we going to do about it? How about, with the help of God, let's go fishing.

We live in an exceedingly mobile society... nothing is nailed down, change is a constant, it is scary out there. But if times of transition and change are good moments to extend our nets in the name of Jesus, what might we do? Let's go fishing!

What makes fish want to swim our way? The bait. And how do the fish get hold of the bait? They get it when we bring it to them, so let's go fishing.

But suppose we are not very good at preparing our hook, or heaven forbid, our bait is bad? No problem. The witness of both scripture and history is that God can use some strange bait to get the fishing done. Not knowing how or being afraid of doing it incorrectly is no excuse, let's just do it. Let's go fishing.

Finally, remember patience. God does not work according to our Timex, even in getting fish to respond to our efforts. Stick with the program. Do not let discouragement keep you from it. Get up. Get on with it. Let's go fishing.

One day, long ago, Jesus said to some friends, "Follow me, and I will make you fish for people." They dropped what they were doing and came along. Now Jesus says to twenty-first-century friends, "Follow me and I will make *you* fish for people." Our response? How about, "Okay, Lord. Let's do it. Let's go fishing."

An ancient legend recounts the return of Jesus to glory after his time on earth. Even in heaven he bore the marks of his earthly pilgrimage with its cruel cross and shameful death. The angel Gabriel approached him and said, "Master, you suffered terribly down there. Do they know and appreciate how much you loved them and what you did for them?"

Jesus replied, "Oh, no! Not yet. Right now only a handful of people in Palestine know."

But Gabriel was perplexed. He asked, "Then how will people learn of what have you done and your love for them?"

Jesus said, "I have asked Andrew and Peter, James and John, and a few more friends to tell others about me. Those who are told will tell others in turn. And my story will be spread to the farthest reaches of the globe. Ultimately, all of humankind will have heard."

Gabriel frowned and looked rather skeptical. He knew what poor stuff humans were made of. He said, "Yes, but what if Andrew, Peter, James, and John grow weary? What if the people who come after them forget? What if they just fail to tell? What is your alternate plan?"

Jesus answered, "I have no other plan."[39] Hmm.

Amen!

---

39. James S. Hewett, *Illustrations Unlimited* (Wheaton, IL: Tyndale House Publishers, Inc, 1988), 256.

Epiphany 4

Mark 1:21-28

We Need Another Miracle

Do you believe in miracles? *Psychology Today* reports of a study that surveyed almost 36,000 Americans, aged eighteen to seventy-plus-years-old, and found that 78% of people under the age of thirty believed in miracles versus 79% among those older than thirty (Pew Research Center, 2010). With respect to religious affiliation, 83% of those who were affiliated believed in miracles in contrast to 55% of respondents who were unaffiliated. Although people from all religions believe in miracles, over 80% of those with Protestant and Catholic affiliations endorsed this belief.[40] The overwhelming majority of us believe that God intervenes in everyday life.

I believe in miracles. I confess that my modern mindset makes me skeptical about some claims for miracles, but scripture makes very plain that some things happen for which there is no explanation but the supernatural.

Our gospel lesson today is one such story, a miracle story. Actually, I think there are two miracles here — the one of the healing of the deranged man, but the other of the way Jesus was received. As the text has it, "when the sabbath came, he entered the synagogue and taught. They were astounded at his teaching, for he taught them as one having authority, and not as the scribes" (Matthew 1:21). The scribes? They were the ones who studied Jewish law most diligently; they were the ones who helped faithful people determine what was right and wrong behavior. For example, they were the ones who interpreted the commandments such as no work on the sabbath — they defined what was work and what was not. For example, under the general no work law, the scribes solemnly set down, as a by-law, that while a woman could have a ribbon sewn onto her dress, it must not be merely pinned on. If it were only pinned, it was not secure enough to be considered a part of the dress, and in wearing the ribbon with a pin, she was carrying

40. Shoba Sreenivasan, "Do you Believe in Miracles?" *Psychology Today* (blog) December 15, 2017, https://www.psychologytoday.com/us/blog/emotional-nourishment/201712/do-you-believe-in-miracles.

a burden. Under the same heading, it was decreed that false teeth were not to be worn on the sabbath... they were a burden. A woman was not allowed to use a mirror on the sabbath to prevent the sin of reaping. Reaping is work. You see, they were concerned that she would see a gray hair and pull it out and pulling out gray hairs was reaping.[41] Crazy. This was the work of the scribes.

Scribal authority came following years and years of study. Now folks were listening to Jesus — a relatively young whipper-snapper — and crediting him in the same way... or even more. Young folks normally are not listened to that way — even today.

Are you familiar with the name Greta Thunberg? Greta is a young Swedish environmental activist who is credited with raising global awareness to the risks posed by climate change, and with holding politicians to account for their lack of action on the climate crisis. In August 2018, at fifteen years of age, Greta took time off from school to demonstrate outside the Swedish parliament, holding up a sign calling for stronger climate action. Soon, other students engaged in similar protests in their own communities. Together they organized a school climate strike movement, under the name Fridays for Future. People actually listened to her at fifteen years old. That is amazing.

Back to the text — the second miracle — the healing of the man with the unclean spirit. Now most of us in the educated, scientifically advanced world would describe this account as an ancient way of diagnosing some unnamed mental illness. Okay. But please be aware that in many parts of the world even today, Christians have no difficulty whatsoever in a belief in spirits, whether clean or unclean, and this old preacher has been around long enough to hold my tongue before going, Tsk, tsk. As you have learned of me before, with Shakespeare I respect the truth of, "There are more things in heaven and earth than are dreamed of in your philosophy..."[42]

The man cries out right in the middle of the service, "What have you to do with us, Jesus of Nazareth? Have you come to destroy us? I know who you are, the holy one of God." Wait a minute. Where are the ushers? Get this guy out of here! But Jesus apparently holds up his hand to stop anyone from tackling this intruder. Instead, he addresses the spirit saying, "Be silent, and come out of him!" And, bingo, the unclean spirit, convulsing him and crying with a loud voice, came out of him.

41. David E. Leininger, God of Justice: A Look at the Ten Commandments for the 21st Century, (Lima, OH: CSS Publishing, 2007), 41.
42 Hamlet. 1.5, 167-168.

A miracle. The question comes again, "Do you believe in miracles?" The gospel writers all do. In fact, they all present the story of Jesus in terms of miracles. Mark has this story, Matthew and Luke begin with the miracle of Jesus' birth, John starts Jesus off with the changing of the water into wine at the wedding in Cana. And the miracles continue throughout the accounts. Do you believe in miracles?

My dictionary defines a miracle as "an effect or extraordinary event in the physical world that surpasses all known human or natural powers and is ascribed to a supernatural cause."[43] I would emphasize the phrase "all known human or natural powers," with the key word being *known*. For example, who in biblical times could have envisioned airline flight, telephones, microwave ovens, instantaneous world-wide communication, walking on the moon, for that matter indoor plumbing or electric lights, any other modern convenience that you and I take completely for granted? It was Montaigne who said, "Miracles arise from our ignorance of nature, not from nature itself."[44]

My son is a US Air Force officer and he has, over the course of his career, been assigned to stations all over the world. No matter where he has been, his mother and I have been able to communicate with him, even face to face, electronically. We had Facetime. How does that work? I have no idea, but it surely does and we take it all in stride. To me, that is nothing short of *miraculous*.

If you happened to notice the dedication of this volume, you would have encountered three names: Noah, Ryan, and Davis. They are three young boys who have enriched the lives of their Mommy and Daddy and most especially their Kiki and PopPop in ways that ways that are completely beyond words. Yes, we know where they come from, but even though we know the physical details about their existence, they are *miracles* to us.

It has been said that, "You're not a realist unless you believe in miracles." That quote has been credited to former Israeli Prime Minister David Ben-Gurion, Egyptian President Anwar Sadat and who knows whomever else. But for anyone who knows the least bit about Middle Eastern history, to suggest that the Israeli-Egyptian Peace Treaty of 1979 could not possibly be anything short of a miracle.

The point is there are lots of miracles out there already, but I would also insist there are lots of unclean spirits out there of many shapes and

43. *Dictionary.com, s.v.* "miracle (*n.*), https://www.dictionary.com/browse/miracleset, February 10, 2020.
44. Frank Mead, ed., *The Encyclopedia of Religious Quotations*, (Old Tappan, NJ: Fleming H. Revell Co., 1976), 458.

sizes that in our own generation are threats. And one of those that really lives up to the name is our climate. It has most assuredly gotten more and more unclean in our own generation.

Carbon emissions are holding in warm temperatures; fires in places like the Amazon rainforest which has been called "the lungs of the world" because of its capacity to minimize the dangers of CO2 are a looming disaster. The trapped heat exacerbates western wildfires. The alternating challenges of drought and flooding have made sustainable farming impossible in areas where self-support used to be possible, resulting in folks leaving their homes as refugees seeking simply the opportunity to create a life. As the planet's relentlessly warming oceans expand and great glaciers and ice sheets melt into the seas, the saltwater continues to rise which threatens everything from the ability to harvest seafood to the well-being of hundreds of millions of people living along the coasts. Since 1900, sea levels have, on average, gone up around eight inches, and this rate is increasing.

For decades, the oceans have served as a crucial buffer against global warming, soaking up roughly a quarter of the carbon dioxide that humans emit from power plants, factories and cars, and absorbing more than 90% of the excess heat trapped on earth by carbon dioxide and other greenhouse gases. Without that protection, the land would be heating much more rapidly. But the oceans themselves are becoming hotter and less oxygen-rich as a result. If humans keep pumping greenhouse gases into the atmosphere at an increasing rate, the risks to human food security and coastal communities will increase sharply, particularly since marine ecosystems are already facing threats from plastic pollution, unsustainable fishing practices and other man-made stresses.

"We are an ocean world, run and regulated by a single ocean, and we are pushing that life support system to its very limits through heating, deoxygenation and acidification." This all comes from a report which was written by more than 100 international experts and is based on more than 7,000 studies, represents the most extensive look to date at the effects of climate change on oceans, ice sheets, mountain snowpack, and permafrost.[45]

This is not new information. We have known about the problem for years. Elsewhere in this volume I wrote about my daughter's kindergarten class studying the destruction of the rainforest and my sweetie's prayer

45. Brad Plumer, "The World's Oceans are in Danger, Major Climate Change Report Warns," *New York Times* (September 25, 2019). https://www.nytimes.com/2019/09/25/climate/climate-change-oceans-united-nations.html.

urging God to kill the perpetrators. This was a generation ago. The truth is we have the ability to fix things. Back in the 1970s we got the word that there was a hole that had developed in the ozone layer of our atmosphere and it was caused by, of all things, the chlorofluorocarbons in our hairspray and our refrigeration systems. We learned of the problem and we fixed it. A *miracle*? Perhaps. But the truth is we have the smarts to do that sort of thing, to make miracles happen.

As to the problems caused by our excessive reliance on fossil fuels, we are working on that as well, but at a speed that makes the tortoise look like a track star. The problem is money and the fact that money has bought off our politicians to keep them from insisting on the changes the world needs. As far back as two centuries ago James Madison, the man who would come to be known as the Father of the Constitution, wrote, "Most of our political evils may be traced to our commercial ones."[46] For Christians, the issue is more than just financial, it is profoundly theological. We believe that God entrusted humanity with a stewardship responsibility toward the earth (Genesis 1:28-31). We have no right to ignore that.

We spoke of Greta Thunberg earlier. In September of 2019, now at the ripe old age of sixteen (can you say driver's license?), Greta addressed the Climate Action Summit at the beginning of the United Nations General Assembly meeting in New York City. She was exceedingly blunt. She said, "My message is that we'll be watching you. This is all wrong. I shouldn't be up here. I should be back in school on the other side of the ocean. Yet you all come to us young people for hope. How dare you! You have stolen my dreams and my childhood with your empty words. And yet I'm one of the lucky ones. People are suffering. People are dying. Entire ecosystems are collapsing. We are in the beginning of a mass extinction, and all you can talk about is money and fairy tales of eternal economic growth. How dare you!" [47]Wow.

Back to the text. We remember what happened. "The unclean spirit, convulsing [the man] and crying with a loud voice, came out of him. They were all amazed, and they kept on asking one another, 'What is this? A new teaching — with authority! He commands even the unclean spirits, and they obey him.'" The truth is, Lord, we need another miracle, for Greta's sake and our own.

Dr. Kate Marvel is a climate scientist at NASA's Goddard Institute for Space Studies. She says there are a lot of things we're really sure

46. Http//founders-archives.gov/documents/jefferson/01-09-02-0301
47. Greta Thurnberg, Speech at United Nations, *USA Today* (September 24, 2019).

about... We're sure sea levels are rising. Scientists are also sure that greenhouse gases — notably carbon dioxide — are trapping heat on the planet, downpours are getting more intense, and rising temperatures are driving increasingly extreme Western wildfires.[48] But she adds,

"I am a scientist, which means I believe in miracles. I live on one. We are improbable life on a perfect planet. A flower in a garden is an exquisite thing, rooted in soil formed from old rocks broken by weather. It breathes in sunlight and carbon dioxide and conjures its food as if by magic. For the flower to exist, a confluence of extraordinary things must happen. It needs land and air and light and water, all in the right proportion, and all at the right time. Pick it, isolate it, and watch it wither. Flowers, like people, cannot grow alone."[49]

A miracle. But the truth, Dr. Marvel, is that, considering the current circumstances, we do need another miracle.

Rachel Held Evans is a voice that the church no longer hears. Sadly, at a far too young age, she died of a severe allergic reaction to an antibiotic that was being used to treat the flu. She was especially insightful as to the church's outreach to millennials like her and was able to identify what might make the church more attractive and inviting to her generation. She wrote, "We're tired of the culture wars, tired of Christianity getting entangled with party politics and power. Millennials want to be known for what we're for, not just what we're against. We don't want to choose between science and religion or between our intellectual integrity and our faith. Instead, we long for our churches to be safe places to doubt, to ask questions, and to tell the truth, even when it's uncomfortable. We want to talk about the tough stuff — biblical interpretation, religious pluralism, sexuality, racial reconciliation, and social justice — but without predetermined conclusions or simplistic answers. We want to bring our whole selves through the church doors, without leaving our hearts and minds behind, without wearing a mask."[50] This climate problem is an issue that resonates. We need a miracle, please. And if you think this one might be too big, think about what happened on that first Easter. Or the one that started it all in the first place.

48. Mark Kaufman, "NASA Scientist Kate Marvel Lays Out the Unpleasant Realities of Rising Seas," *Mashable* (September 22, 2019)..
49. "Climate Change: Abandon All Hope?" *This Week* (September 27, 2019).
50. Rachel Held Evans, *Searching For Sunday: Loving,Leaving and Finding the Church*, (Nashville, TN: Nelson Books, 2015), xiii-xiv.

A woman took her sixteen-year-old daughter to the doctor. The doctor said, "Okay, Mrs. Jones, what's the problem?"

The mother said, "It's my daughter, Debbie. She keeps getting these cravings, she's putting on weight, and is sick most mornings."

The doctor gave Debbie a good examination, then turned to the mother and said, "Well, I don't know how to tell you this, but your Debbie is pregnant – about four months, would be my guess."

The mother replied, "Pregnant?! She can't be, she has never ever been left alone with a man! Have you, Debbie?"

Debbie answered, "No mother! I've never even kissed a man!"

The doctor walked over to the window and just stared out it. About five minutes passed and finally the mother said, "Is there something wrong out there doctor?"

The doctor replies, "No, not really, it's just that the last time anything like this happened, a star appeared in the east and three wise men came over the hill. I'll be darned if I'm going to miss it this time!"[51]

Indeed. And, yes, Lord, we need another miracle.

Amen.

51. Mr. FunnyBone quoted in *Bible Illustrator for Windows*, (Hiawatha, Iowa: Parsons Technology, 1994), diskette.

Heroines Of The Faith

I am certain that you Bible scholars have experienced the same phenomenon as I have, namely, that you can read the same passage over and over and over again and find something that strikes you anew each time. Scripture does not change, of course, but *we* change. It is that old saying about not being able to step into the same river twice.

That is my experience with this pericope. In years past, I would have noted the Lord's healing ministry, the way the word spread through the people about this wonder-worker, Jesus' need for respite and prayer, and the like. But this time, I am drawn to the vignette that we find right near the beginning of the passage: "Now Simon's mother-in-law was in bed with a fever, and they told him about her at once. He came and took her by the hand and lifted her up. Then the fever left her, and she began to serve them." (Mark 1:30-31) Years ago, I thought nothing of it, but now... She was sick in bed, Jesus healed her, she got up, and went about playing the perfect hostess. Huh?

It reminds me of the story of the fifteen-year-old boy who came bounding into the house and found his mom in bed. He asked if she were sick or something. He was truly concerned. Mom replied that, as a matter of fact, she didn't feel too well. The son replied, "Well, don't worry a bit about dinner. I'll be happy to carry you down to the stove."[52] Uh-huh.

Years ago, I thought nothing of gender stereotypes, but times change. And I have changed. When I grew up, gender roles were fairly rigid, but no more. When I went to seminary, there were very few women in parish ministry. That is not the case any longer. Gender barriers have come crashing down. There is still discrimination, but every year it declines bit by bit. Good.

The same is certainly true in the secular world. The twenty-first century has seen the Harvard-educated Ellen Johnson-Sirleaf elected as President of Liberia, Africa's first female president. Angela Merkel

---

52. James S. Hewett, *Illustrations Unlimited* (Wheaton: Tyndale House Publishers, Inc, 1988), 378.

has been one of the longest serving chancellors of Germany. Michelle Bachelet was elected president of Chile, the first woman to lead a major Latin American country. Since the 1990s, more than thirty women have become heads of government. In the 1950s there was just one (Suhbaataryn Yanjmaa, president of Mongolia.).

Not just heads of state either. In Iraq, women fill at least 25% of seats in the Parliament because the Iraqi Constitution has a quota requiring it. Overall, fifty countries have quotas for female representation in their legislatures. In many countries, like Sweden, political parties have adopted rules that force them to field a set number of women candidates. However, the lowest female representation by region is in the Arab world, with women making up only 8% of legislatures.[53]

Does all this gender shift make any real difference? Many voters seem to think so. A Gallup poll in Latin America a few years ago found that 62% of people believed that women would do better than men at fighting poverty, 72% favored women for improving education and 53% thought women would make better diplomats.[54] There is growing evidence that, at the very least, where women make up a significant percentage of government, they tend to hold priorities that are different from men's. The World Economic Forum found, in a study of just three countries, that women wanted more money for health care, education and social welfare, and less for the military. Across the globe, women are perceived as less corrupt. Interesting stuff.

This is consistent with growing evidence at a grassroots level that women are better recipients of aid than men. Around the world, if you give cash to a mother, she tends to use it to invest in children's health and education. (A man, on the other hand, will often take it and head to the local watering hole.) "Studies from Brazil show that survival possibilities of a child increase by 20% if the income is in the hands of the mother rather than the father." So says the World Bank.[55]

There is another perceived difference between men and women. A few years ago, an article appeared in Foreign Affairs in which it was argued that "aggression, violence, war, and intense competition for dominance... are more closely associated with men than women." The conclusion was that "a world run by women would follow different

53. "Woman in National Parliments," *Archive.ipu* (February 1, 2019). archives.ipu.org/wmn-e/classif.htm/
54. Johanna Godoy, "Latin America: Signs of Progress," *Gallup* (March 8, 2019). news.gallup.com/poll/247199/latin-america-signe-progress-change-takes-time.aspx.
55. Daimen de Walque, "Should Cash Transfers be Systematically Paid to Mothers?," *World Bank Blog* (July 6, 2016). blogs.worldbank.org/developmenttalk/should-cash-transfers-be-systematically-paid-mothers.

rules."[56] That may be open to question considering that Margaret Thatcher, Golda Meir, and Indira Gandhi, to name just a few, did not hesitate to lead their nations in war.

In the church, in my own denomination, the Presbyterian Church (USA), it was almost 100 years ago (1930) that our General Assembly passed Resolution B voting to ordain women as elders and the next year five women were elected as commissioners to that Assembly. Some men feared women would take over the church. Some women wondered why the men would think the women wanted it. Another 25 years would go by before the first woman was ordained to the Presbyterian ministry. In 1956, Margaret Towner became the first woman ordained to the Ministry of Word and Sacrament in the United Presbyterian Church.

Margaret left a career as a medical photographer at the Mayo Clinic to study education at Syracuse University prior to accepting the job as Director of Christian Education at the East Genesee, New York Church. She then pursued the three-year Bachelor of Divinity Degree at Union Theological Seminary in New York, believing that such training would be helpful in her work in Christian Education. She moved to First Church, Allentown, Pennsylvania and she flourished. It was suggested that she pursue ordination to the ministry, and, sho' 'nuff, she became the first female pastor in our denomination.

Towner's ordination did not bring her equality with males. There was and, sadly, still is, a "stained glass ceiling" in the church that denies full equality. Perhaps typical was a remark at the presbytery meeting following Margaret's official entrance into ministry: one man asked, "What do we do now, address everyone as brethren and sistern?"[57] Why not? As anyone with eyes can see, the number of women ministers in mainline congregations has increased exponentially in recent years and there is no indication that the trend will change anytime soon.

So saying, I would love to report that the church has taken the lead in ensuring gender equality. Not really. There are still some parts of the church that have a problem with that, and that even with the contrary witness of scripture. In the Hebrew Bible, we have the creation of Eve as a "helpmate" or partner (not simply assistant) to Adam in the Garden. Wags (short for Skalawags) have pictured the angels asking God, why this new creation and God responding, "I saw my first result and figured I could do better." Uh-huh. There are lots of great names in scripture —

56. Francis Fukuyama, "Woman and the Evolution of World Politics," *Foreign Affairs* (September 1998). foreignaffairs.com/articles/1998-09-1/woman-and-evolution-world-politics
57. James H. Smylie, "Women Ministers (1955-1966) and Margaret Towner," *The Presbyterian Outlook*, (February 6, 2006)..

Rebekah, Sarah, Rachel, Hannah, Ruth, and Queen Esther. In the New Testament we have Mary, of course. Women were the first witnesses to the resurrection. In the early church we find faithful ladies like Dorcas and Lydia. Quite frankly, from the first day to this day, if it were not for the women, there would be no church. It is that simple.

Think of some of them. Think of Anne Hutchinson, a heroine for her insistence on religious freedom in America.[58] Anne emigrated from England with her family in 1634 as part of the Puritan movement that was dissatisfied with the Church of England. They were searching for religious freedom in the new world, but the freedom on these shores was not as free as some might have hoped. The Massachusetts Bay Colony was organized as a rigid theocracy that demanded strict adherence to a code of conduct and did not tolerate dissent of any kind, and certainly not from a woman, because it was widely believed that women did not have the native capacity for spiritual discernment (they should keep themselves only to be wives and mothers).

Anne Hutchinson must have been a remarkable individual because she attracted other women from the colony to her home-based religious discussions and Bible studies. Governor John Winthrop in his diary called her an "American Jezebel." He believed women should not be behaving like this. Anne and her family were banished from Massachusetts for her boldness and settled in what is now Rhode Island, then moved to Long Island. Anne Hutchinson, a woman of courage who surely qualifies as a heroine of the faith.

Another woman of great courage was Sojourner Truth. Born a slave named Isabella around 1797, she became a crusader for emancipation for the slaves and new rights for women. She was converted in a dramatic fashion when she says the Spirit of Jesus came to her to express his love and say to her, "I know you! I know you!" When given her freedom in New York in 1827, Isabella went to New York City where she worked cooking, cleaning, and caring for the sick. Then God gave her a new name, Sojourner Truth, and she traveled throughout the country speaking against the sin of slavery.

Often clergymen challenged her right to speak to men — women were to keep silent. Once confronted by some males in the audience, she replied:

58. Anne Adams, "Anne Hutchinson: Advocate for Religious Freedom," *History's Women.* http://www.historyswomen.com/womenoffaith/AnneHutchinson.htm.

"Some say woman can't have as much rights as a man cause Christ wasn't a woman. Where did Christ come from? From God and a woman. Men had nothing to do with him. If the first woman God ever made was strong enough to turn the world upside down all alone, all women together ought to be able to turn it back and get it right side up again and now that they are asking to do it, men better let' em."[59]

You go, girl! There are other heroines. There was Amy Carmichael, the missionary to India near the end of the 19th century who founded the Dohnavur Fellowship, which became a haven for homeless children, especially girls who had escaped from temple prostitution.[60] She was even given "temple babies," infants that were born of the temple prostitutes, to raise in her "home." Amy Carmichael was an inspiration and heroine to, not only those girls she rescued in India, but who knows how many others through her extensive writings.

There is Donaldina Cameron in San Francisco. In 1882, Congress passed the first of three Chinese exclusion acts which prevented all but a few privileged classes of Chinese men from sending for their families in China. Single men could not send for Chinese wives, nor did the law permit them to marry non-Chinese wives. The small ratio of Chinese women to men bred a rampant prostitution market. To meet the demand, Chinese girls and young women, mostly from Canton, were bought, kidnapped, or coerced into coming to America. Once in the country, these girls were sold for one of two purposes — those in their teens were pressed into prostitution; little ones were sold for household servants called Mui Tsai's. As they got older, they were frequently sold into prostitution as well. It was the rescue of these Mui Tsai's and prostitutes that was Donaldina Cameron's mission. She is credited with breaking the back of the Chinese slave trade in the US and the rescue and education of nearly 3,000 girls — an amazing woman.[61]

In our own day we were blessed by the presence of another incredible heroine of the faith. She was called Agnes by her Albanian parents but the world came to know her as Mother Teresa, a name she chose as she became a nun in honor of St. Teresa of Lisieux, patron saint of foreign missionaries.[62] From what has been called a "life-changing encounter

59. Bill J. Leonard, *Word of God Across the Ages*, (Nashville: Broadman Press, 1981), 71.
60. "Amy Carmichael: Founder of Dohnavur Fellowship," *History's Women*. http://www. historyswomen.com/womenoffaith/amy.html.
61. Vicki Thomas, "Cameron, Donaldina: Missionary, Social Worker and Youth Advocate," *Encyclopedia of San Francisco*, 2003. http://www.sfhistoryencyclopedia.com/articles/c/ cameronDonaldina.html.
62. Anne Adams, "Mother Teresa: Compassionate Servant of God," *History's Women*. http:// www.historyswomen.com/womenoffaith/MotherTeresa_000.htm.

with the Living Presence of the Will of God" on a train journey in September, 1946 came a unique ministry to the poorest of the poor in India.

"There is a terrible hunger for love," she wrote. "We all experience that in our lives — the pain, the loneliness. We must have the courage to recognize it. The poor you may have right in your own family. Find them. Love them. Put your love for them in living action. For in loving them, you are loving God."

The work of Mother Teresa and the Missionaries of Charity received much international notice and acclaim, the most prestigious, of course, her receiving of the Nobel Peace Prize in 1979. The comment was made when she received it that "her labor made her so worthy that, in reality, she gave honor to the prize, rather than the other way around!" As time went on, she confessed her own doubts and struggles with faith, but she persevered, and her work has wonderfully survived her. She was truly a heroine of the faith.

And then there was the mother-in-law of Simon Peter - in bed with a fever. Jesus came, took her by the hand and lifted her up. The fever left her, and she began to serve. Good lady.

These are true heroines of the faith. There have been so many. No doubt, you could name several that might be known only to you. Fortunately, for almost a half century now, I have been blessed to be married to one of them. Thank you, Christie.

An old story: Three guys were out having a relaxing day fishing. Out of the blue, they caught a mermaid who begged to be set free in return for granting each of them a wish. Now one of the guys just doesn't believe it, and said, "Okay, if you can really grant wishes, then double my IQ."

The mermaid said, "Done." Suddenly, the guy started reciting Shakespeare flawlessly and analyzing it with amazing insight.

The second guy was so blown away that he said to the mermaid, "Triple my IQ."

The mermaid said, "Done." The guy started to spout out all the mathematical solutions to problems that had been stumping all the scientists of varying fields – physics, chemistry, and more.

The last guy was so enthralled with the changes in his friends, that he said to the mermaid, "Quintuple my IQ."

The mermaid looked at him and said, "You know, I normally don't try to change people's minds when they make a wish, but I really wish you would reconsider."

The guy said, "Nope, I want you to increase my IQ times five, and if you don't do it, I won't set you free."

"Please," said the mermaid, "You don't know what you're asking... it will change your entire view on the universe... won't you ask for something else... a million dollars, anything?" But no matter what the mermaid said, the guy insisted on having his IQ increased by five times its usual power. So, the mermaid sighed and said, "Done."

And he became a woman.[63]

We love you, ladies. God bless you for who you are and all that you do.

Amen!

63. "Mermaid Granst a Wish...," *Kent.Edu.* math.kent.edu/-mtackett/chuckles/mermaidwish. html.

Transfiguration of the Lord

Mark 9:2-9

The View From The Mountaintop

The transfiguration of the Lord. An important day on the calendar of the church, and one that regularly falls near another important day on the secular calendar of America, the birthday of the man who has been called America's greatest president, Abraham Lincoln. We have heard the old aphorism about some being born great, some achieving greatness, and some having greatness thrust upon them. Abraham Lincoln can surely lay claim to, at least, the last two of those.

Lincoln has always fascinated me. Many of you as well, no doubt. In fact, he is now seen as so important a figure that one contemporary historian notes that there are currently more books in the English language about Lincoln than about anyone else except Jesus and Shakespeare.[64]

He became our president in 1861 and served throughout at a most inauspicious time. On Lincoln's first day in office he was greeted with a dispatch from Fort Sumter letting him know that the Union troops would have difficulty holding out for much longer unless they were resupplied. And, as we all know, they did *not* hold out. His last day in office came as a result of what might be called the "final shot" of the Civil War — the one fired by John Wilkes Booth.

The lines between Lincoln and his Confederate counterpart, Jefferson Davis, were clearly drawn. Lincoln wrote, "Between him and us the issue is distinct, simple, and inflexible. It is an issue which can only be tried by war, and decided by victory."[65] There was no middle ground — too bad. The war that resulted was the most violent event in American history. The 620,000 soldiers killed almost equals the number of American fighters killed in all our country's other wars combined.[66]

It was a horrible time. In the north, Henry Ward Beecher was pastor of Brooklyn's Plymouth Congregational Church, the most influential

64. James M. McPherson, *Abraham Lincoln and The Second American Revolution*, (New York: Oxford University Press, 1990), 68.
65. James M. McPherson, *Abraham Lincoln and the Second American Revolution (New York: Oxford University Press*, 1990), 124.
66. James M. McPherson, *Abraham Lincoln and The Second American Revolution*, (New York: Oxford University Press, 1990), 88.

pulpit in the land. When he spoke at ceremonies marking the recapture of Fort Sumter, Beecher made clear what he thought the conflict meant in the eye of God: "I charge the whole guilt of this war upon the ambitious, educated, plotting leaders of the south... A day will come when God will reveal judgment and arraign these mighty miscreants... And then these guiltiest and most remorseless traitors... shall be whirled aloft and plunged downward forever and ever in an endless retribution."[67] Lordy!

In the south, Robert Lewis Dabney was almost as prominent as Beecher in the North. A Presbyterian defender of scripture and of traditional confessions, he was even more orthodox than Beecher. During the war Dabney served on the staff of General Stonewall Jackson; afterward he presided over seminaries in South Carolina and in Texas. Yet from wherever Dabney viewed the conflict, his opinion was the same. The war, he thought, was "caused deliberately" by evil abolitionists who persecuted the south "with calculated malice." When fellow southerners asked him to soften his views on denominational colleagues in the North, Dabney had only these chilling words: "What! Forgive those people who have invaded our country, burned our cities, destroyed our homes, slain our young men, and spread desolation and ruin over our land?! No, I do not forgive them."[68] For the rest of his life, Dr. Dabney refused to accept the *un*-acceptability of human slavery; for that matter, he was equally unaccepting of women in the pulpit.[69]

As to Mr. Lincoln, in a way, it is surprising to look back on him as a great wartime leader because story after story has come down to us concerning his compassionate nature (pardons for deserters, help for needy southern families, and mercy for the Confederacy at Appomattox). At the beginning of the war he was convinced that firmness should be tempered with restraint. Lincoln promised that while suppressing the rebels, Union troops would avoid "any devastation, any destruction of, or interference with, property, or any disturbance of peaceful citizens."[70]

As time went on, of course, events dictated a change in that limited strategy. Lincoln himself wrote to General Sheridan and congratulated him on the scorched earth of the Shenandoah Valley. The President did the same in a letter to General Sherman after his devastation of South Carolina and Georgia. War (then and now) is never as clean as might be

---

67. Ed. Robert R, Mathisen, "Good Men and Angels Will Cry Out," *The Routledge Sourcebook of Religion and the American Civil War* (New York: Routledge, 2015), 447.
68. Mark Noll, *The Puzzling faith of Abraham Lincoln*, http://www.christianitytoday.com/ch/1992/issue33/3311.html.
69. http://www.biblebb.com/files/RD-001WP.htm.
70. McPherson, ibid., 75.

hoped. Innocent people suffer!

Lincoln suffered too. He had his own private war with depression which he battled with a widely-recognized sense of humor. There was a story that circulated around Washington during those years concerning him and Jefferson Davis. Two pious Quaker ladies were discussing the relative merits and prospects of the two leaders. One said, "I think Davis will succeed because he is a praying man."

The other replied, "But so is Lincoln."

The first responded, "Yes, but when Abraham prays, the Lord will think he's joking."[71]

Once at a cabinet meeting, the president read aloud from a humorous book. The cabinet members were amazed; not one of them even smiled. "Gentlemen," Lincoln asked with a sigh, "why don't you laugh? With the fearful strain that is upon me day and night, if I did not laugh, I should die."

Abraham Lincoln knew the depths of despair. During one particularly trying time he wrote a friend and said, "I am now the most miserable man living. If what I feel were equally distributed to the whole human family, there would not be one cheerful face on the earth."[72]

Of course, the president was the recipient of all sorts of advice to help him with his momentous decisions (just as any president ever is). Many of the arguments were based on religion and the unshakeable certainty that God wanted whatever problem was being discussed handled this way (whichever way the speaker was heading). Lincoln said, "In great contests each party claims to act in accordance with the will of God. Both may be, and one must be *wrong*. God cannot be for, and against, the same thing at the same time." He also wrote, "I hope it will not be irreverent for me to say, that if it is probable that God would reveal his will to others on a point so connected with *my* duty, it might be supposed that he would reveal it directly to me... if I can learn what it is, I will do it."[73] Good for you, Abe.

Lincoln's religious training began early. As a young lad he would go to church, hear a sermon, come home, take the younger children out, get on a stump or a log an almost repeat the morning's message word for word. His family said that, not only would he recall the sermon, but he would also mimic accurately the preacher's eccentricities of style

---

71. Clifton Fadiman, Gen. Ed., *The Little, Brown Book of Anecdotes*, (Boston: Little, Brown & Co., 1985), 358.
72. Watson F. Pindell, *Milestones to Immortality* (Baltimore: Role Models, Inc., 1988), 30.
73. Watson F. Pindell, Milestons, *Abraham Lincoln and The Second American Revolution*, (New York: Oxford University Press, 1990) 94.

and voice.[74] Lincoln had his own ideas about what preaching ought to be. Later in life he reportedly said, "I do not like to hear cut and dried sermons. When I hear a man preach I like to see him act as if he were fighting bees!"[75] Glory!

Soon after settling in the White House, the Lincoln family rented a pew in Washington's New York Avenue Presbyterian Church where Mrs. Lincoln became a member. The whole family regularly attended on Sunday mornings. The President also came to the mid-week prayer service, but to avoid office-seekers and contractors who would pester him anytime he appeared in public, Lincoln did not sit with the congregation; instead he used a side entrance and sat in the minister's darkened study with the door slightly ajar so he could hear what was going on. The President said that he always found that listening to people talking *to* God was a greater source of strength than listening to people talking *about* God.[76]

Concerning his own profession of faith Lincoln said, "I cannot without mental reservations assent to long and complicated creeds and catechisms. If a church would ask simply for assent to the Savior's statement of the substance of the law: `Thou shalt love the Lord thy God with all thy heart and with all thy soul and with all thy mind and thy neighbor as thyself' — that church would I gladly unite with." Many today would echo that sentiment.

He went on, "Probably it is to be my lot to go on in a twilight, feeling... with him of old time, who, in his need, as I in mine, exclaimed, "Help Thou mine unbelief."[77] Honest Abe was a man of honest faith... and honest doubt.

Those words, "I believe; help my unbelief!" came from another man whose life reflected a mixture of honest faith and doubt. Jesus, Peter, James, and John had come back from the mountaintop experience of our text. It had been a beautiful moment, but now they were back in the world where people fight with each other, the world where little children get sick for no reason, the world where folks get frustrated with their problems, the world where the faith of the mountaintop gives way to the despair and doubt of the valley. The mountaintop experiences are wonderful when they come, but the world where most of us live (and where Abraham Lincoln lived) is the one that hears the loving Dad of an epileptic child at the end of his rope say, "I believe; help my unbelief!

74. Watson F. Pindell, *Milestones*, 8-9.
75. *Milestones*, 42.
76. *Milestones*, 78-79.
77. *Milestones*, 37.

(Mark 9:24)" and we whisper *Amen*.

Lincoln once said, "I have often wished that I was a more devout man than I am. Nevertheless, amid the greatest difficulties of my administration, when I could not see any other resort, I would place my whole reliance in God, knowing that all would go well, and that he would decide for the right."[78] Abraham Lincoln had his honest doubts (as anyone with any sense would — there is no shame in that), but he was a man of more faith than perhaps even he knew.

One of the best preachers of Lincoln's day, Phillips Brooks, in a memorial sermon after the assassination said, "He [Lincoln] fed us faithfully and truly. He fed us with counsel when we were in doubt, with inspiration when we sometimes faltered, with caution when we would be rash... He fed hungry souls all over the country with sympathy and consolation... He fed us with solemn, solid truths... Best of all, he fed us with a reverent and genuine religion. He spread before us the love and fear of God just in that shape in which we need them most, and out of his faithful service of a higher Master, who of us has not taken and eaten and grown strong? At the last, behold Lincoln standing with hand reached out to feed the South with mercy and the North with charity, and the whole land with peace, when the Lord who had sent him called him and his work was done!"[79]

"...when the Lord who had sent him called him and his work was done!" There is an affirmation of providence in that sentence that sends us back to our scripture lesson. We find this strange mountaintop scene, the Transfiguration of the Lord. Jesus and three of his closest friends had climbed up to pray and rest. But while they were there, Jesus was "transfigured" — as far as Peter, James, and John could see, he "glowed," something they had never encountered before. But if that were not enough, two of the greatest heroes of ancient religious history, Moses and Elijah, the great law-giver and the great prophet, appeared as well... paying their respects to one who was even greater than they. Finally, a voice came from the cloud that surrounded them up there, the voice of God: "This is my Son, the beloved; listen to him!" It affirmed for those disciples (if they had any lingering doubts) that this Jesus whom they had come to love and trust was more than a man — he was divine. A mountaintop experience if there ever was one!

True, there would be a time to come back from the mountain. Life is

---

78. *Milestones*, 122.
79. Phillips Brooks, "Abraham Lincoln," *Twenty Centuries of Great Preaching,* Volume 6, (Waco, Texas: Word, 1971), 135.

lived in the valley and that is where we find that heartbreaking scene of the father of an epileptic boy desperately looking for help; fortunately, he finds the help in Jesus. For Peter, James, and John, life in the valley would never be the same again. Despite the fights and the fears and the failures, all the things that would contribute to a lack of faith, these three had seen God's future, the future that an early Christian hymn would describe as a time when every knee would bow and every tongue confess that Jesus Christ is Lord... a time of no more sorrow, no more sickness, no more tears, no more pain, no more war... a time when every valley would be exalted and every mountain made a plain. Peter, James, and John had seen who was in charge, and with the lyric of the spiritual that slaves of Lincoln's day would sing, know, "He's got the whole world in *His* hands."

That day on the mountain, that moment in the close presence of God, changed those men, just as these moments in worship, the moments when we feel God especially near, can change you and me. Yes, with the father of the gospel story we cry out, "Lord, I believe; help my unbelief." But with Peter, James and John we glimpse the future and, with eyes of faith, see a better day. "Glory, Glory, Hallelujah!"

Mr. Lincoln saw a better day and just one month before his death challenged his America and ours: "With malice toward none, with charity for all, with firmness in the right as God gives us to see the right, let us finish the work we are in, to bind up the nation's wounds, to care for him who shall have borne the battle, and for his widow and his orphans, to do all which may achieve and cherish a just and lasting peace among ourselves and all nations."[80] Oh yes, Mr. Lincoln. Oh yes, Lord!

Amen!

---

80. Abraham Lincoln, "Second Inaugural Address," *Masterpieces of American Eloquence,* (New York: Christian Herald, 1900), 239.

www.ingramcontent.com/pod-product-compliance
Lightning Source LLC
Chambersburg PA
CBHW032024090426
42741CB00006B/730